W9-BDK-348

What a theologically savvy and empathy-embracing book for today's church! Reading *A Church Called Tov* reminded me of why I love the church, and how that affection can also mean telling the truth about her missteps and broken pieces. In a world of high profile failures and scandals, this book offers a prophetic reimagining of the Acts 2 church. It is hopeful, relevant, and encouraging.

MARY DEMUTH, author of *We Too: How the Church Can Respond Redemptively to the Sexual Abuse Crisis*

It is tragic that a book like this has to be written. However, if good can come of tragedy, this book is a testimony to that. In this volume, Scot and Laura have given the church a way of identifying, naming, and addressing toxic church cultures with a view to retraining our thinking to create cultures of goodness and healthy churches. It is full of wisdom, insight, and truthful exegesis which brings its own light. It is a gift to leaders, pastors in training, and importantly, victims of abuse who desperately need champions. In my view, this should be essential reading for anyone who has any leadership responsibility in a church.

LUCY PEPPIATT, principal, Westminster Theological Centre, Cheltenham, UK

This profoundly important book addresses the problem of toxic church culture and shows how we change it. It is brave, thoughtful, and transformational. The answers it offers are woven around the key Hebrew word *tov*, which means good—and so much more. If you have been wounded by your experience of church, you should read this book. If you cannot imagine how church wounds people, you should read this book. It is profound, compassionate, and—sadly—timely.

PAULA GOODER, New Testament scholar and Canon Chancellor of St Paul's Cathedral in London

If the church is going to become what she was designed to be, women must be at equal places of responsibility, authority, and influence in all spaces. If there has ever been a time to write a better story—a *tov* story—it is now! The broken stories in this book offer a beautiful transformational pathway forward. I wish this book weren't necessary, but it is imperative for leaders committed to integrity and creating a better future.

APRIL L. DIAZ, founder, Ezer + Co.

A Church Called Tov is a desperately needed book, full of eye-opening truths. The church is supposed to be, and *can* be, a place of goodness, not toxicity. Scot and Laura help us discern the difference. It is clear they have seen and understand both sides and therefore can serve as guides to help us see what is good and avoid what is evil. I hope this work spreads through every church.

WADE MULLEN, author of *Something's Not Right*

In a time when scores of people who grew up in the church are walking away wounded, disillusioned, and understandably cynical about a culture that seldom reflects the Jesus it claims to love and follow, Scot McKnight brings us much-needed hope. He does this by helping the reader diagnose and explain what creates and fosters the toxicity that is so pervasive within our modern Christian culture. Fortunately, Scot doesn't stop there. He follows up his diagnosis with an informed and practical wisdom that empowers and equips us cynics to understand how the church can actually become what it was created to be . . . the community of true health, safe refuge, and genuine hope for the weary and the wounded. In other words, the reflection of the Jesus. I'm grateful that *A Church Called Tov* helped me begin deconstructing my own cynicism about the church. Baby steps forward. Thanks, Scot!

BOZ TCHIVIDJIAN, victim rights attorney and founder of GRACE (Godly Response to Abuse in the Christian Environment)

SCOT McKNIGHT
LAURA BARRINGER

A CHURCH CALLED

TOV

Forming a Goodness Culture That Resists Abuses of Power and Promotes Healing

MOMENTUM®

The Tyndale nonfiction imprint

Library of Congress Cataloging-in-Publication Data
Names: McKnight, Scot, author. | Barringer, Laura, author.
Title: A church called Tov : forming a goodness culture that resists abuses
   of power and promotes healing / Scot McKnight and Laura Barringer.
Description: Carol Stream, Illinois : Tyndale House Publishers, 2020. |
   Includes bibliographical references.
Identifiers: LCCN 2020018427 (print) | LCCN 2020018428 (ebook) | ISBN
   9781496446008 (hardcover) | ISBN 9781496446015 (kindle edition) | ISBN
   9781496446022 (epub) | ISBN 9781496446039 (epub)
Subjects: LCSH: Church. | Sex crimes--Religious aspects--Christianity. |
   Offenses against the person. | Authority--Religious
   aspects--Christianity.
Classification: LCC BV600.3 .M3565 2020 (print) | LCC BV600.3 (ebook) |
   DDC 262/.72--dc23
LC record available at https://lccn.loc.gov/2020018427
LC ebook record available at https://lccn.loc.gov/2020018428

Printed in the United States of America

26   25   24   23   22
 7   6   5   4   3   2

For the Wounded Resisters

✳ ✳ ✳

CONTENTS

FOREWORD

THE CHURCH IS PART OF THE GOOD NEWS OF JESUS. Jesus' mission was not simply to save individuals. He created a people, a community, an institution to bring his enduring light, truth, peace, and goodness into all the world and every part of human society. He built a church, and he calls this church his own—his bride, his body, his people—which is why we confess in the Nicene Creed that we believe in one holy, catholic, and apostolic church. The late Archbishop of Canterbury Michael Ramsey wrote, "We do not know the whole fact of Christ incarnate unless we know his Church, and its life as part of his own life."[1]

And yet, I have been thrown into deep doubt and a crisis of faith from the failures of church leaders. I have wept bitter tears as a powerful male pastor surrounded himself with a tight inner ring of adorers and responded harshly to any he deemed unworthy of his careful affections.

It is clear that the church regularly breaks our hearts, disappoints, and even damages us. Both history and our current headlines reveal a church that can be a deeply flawed, sinful, and unhealthy institution, marred by acts of injustice, corruption, abuse, misogyny, and oppression. The contemporary American church is wrecked with bickering and division, celebrity worship and unaccountable leaders, false and shallow teaching, and a Christian industrial complex formed around greed and vanity.

Yes, the church is part of the good news of Jesus. And the church proclaims the good news of Jesus. But when men and women have only seen churches formed by unhealthy power, celebrity, competitiveness, secrecy, and self-protection, our corporate ecclesial life belies the truth of the gospel. The church can only witness to the truth of Jesus by seeking justice, serving with humility, operating transparently, and confessing and lamenting failures.

So what do we do? How do we seek to embrace the church as the divine organism that Jesus created, without denying the real darkness and danger we find in its very human and fragile institutions?

This book helpfully centers this key challenge: How do we nurture a church culture marked by goodness?

We, as a church, by the power of the Holy Spirit, have to do the hard work of speaking frankly about our sins and failings, repenting actively, and reconstructing a church culture rooted in truth, grace, and transparency. And we need guides for this hard task. Here, Scot McKnight and Laura Barringer serve as two such guides.

Using stories from their own lives and the testimony of victims, they walk us through specific ways the church has failed and the kind of cultures that allow (and even encourage) abuse and the misuse of power.

But they do not stop there. The great virtue of this book is that the authors also show how to help establish church cultures that lead to flourishing, health, and goodness. As they help us navigate the terrain of Christian leadership in the twenty-first century, they skillfully point out the perils and precipices of church life. But they also plot a better course—a way to be *grace dispensers*, people who embody compassion toward the distressed and marginalized, honor the gifts and callings of women, and seek both justice and forgiveness.

What is most helpful about this book is that, while it maintains its theological vision, it never falls into the trap of simply pontificating about what the church is not or could be. This book is deeply personal and profoundly practical. And this is a great gift. These pages contain real-life stories of people and communities. And because of this, we find our own selves, lives, and churches in these pages.

Reading these stories brought to mind the ways I've experienced spiritual abuse and toxic leadership cultures in my own Christian life. It also challenged me to see ways that my own ministry and church culture could be changed and formed to better reflect the holiness and health to which we are called.

It can be easy to cast church abuse in purely individualistic terms—a few "bad apples." But what *A Church Called Tov* shows is that we have a cultural problem in the church that results in patterns of abuse, repeated again and again in different localities, traditions, and ecclesial contexts. Culture change is difficult and requires intentionality. But for those churches and church leaders who aspire to what Jacques Ellul called the "extreme difficulty of incarnating the truth,"[2] Scot McKnight and Laura Barringer dare us to embark on a beautiful path of healing and transformation.

Tish Harrison Warren
Author of Liturgy of the Ordinary: Sacred Practices in Everyday Life

WHERE WE FIND OURSELVES

ON MARCH 23, 2018, my husband and I (Laura) were paying for our dinner at a local restaurant when we received a text message from my parents, with a link to a breaking news story in the *Chicago Tribune*. As I read the headline to Mark—"After Years of Inquiries, Willow Creek Pastor Denies Misconduct Allegations"— we both rolled our eyes in disbelief that someone would accuse Bill Hybels, the founding and senior pastor of Willow Creek Community Church, of sexual misconduct. In the article, the *Tribune* reported accusations from several women of "suggestive comments, extended hugs, an unwanted kiss and invitations to hotel rooms," and "an allegation of a prolonged consensual affair with a married woman who later [retracted] her claim."[1]

"There's no way this is true," I said to Mark. We attended Willow Creek for nearly two decades and always admired Bill Hybels's leadership. We never suspected anything untoward in his behavior, though admittedly at a church the size of Willow Creek, congregants rarely know what's happening behind the curtain. During that twenty-year period, I only spoke to Bill Hybels once, after standing in line to meet him after an evening service. He said, "My daughter knows your family. She speaks highly of you guys."

I continued reading the story aloud as Mark drove us home from the restaurant. When the article mentioned Vonda Dyer, a former director of Willow Creek's vocal ministry, Mark and I looked at each other with incredulity, and I felt a sense of dread begin to grow in the pit of my stomach. Vonda told the *Tribune* that "Hybels called her to his hotel suite on a trip to Sweden in 1998, unexpectedly kissed her and suggested they could lead Willow Creek together."[2]

"Oh no," Mark said. He was silent for a moment before adding, "I've known Vonda for nearly twenty years. This is real. She's telling the truth."

I kept reading. The next woman mentioned was Nancy Beach, who "recounted more than one conversation or interaction she felt was inappropriate during moments alone with Hybels over the years."[3]

Nancy Beach. Another woman of character and integrity. My father has known Nancy for years. As I continued to read, the names were all familiar: John and Nancy Ortberg, Leanne Mellado, Betty Schmidt. These were people we believed to be sincere and honest. Most were family friends, with longstanding connections to Willow Creek as well. Why would they lie? They would have no reason to "collude" to ruin Bill Hybels's reputation, as he suggested in the *Tribune* article.[4] But if the women were telling the truth, then Bill Hybels was not. As we began to grapple with the news, these two competing thoughts proved impossible to reconcile.

* * *

When Laura and Mark arrived home that evening, they called me (Scot) to get my perspective.

"The probabilities are that this story is true," I said to them on the phone.

"How do you know this?" Laura asked.

"I hope I'm wrong," I said. But it's a predictable pattern. And there's very little chance that Vonda Dyer, Nancy Beach, Leanne Mellado, Betty Schmidt, *and* Nancy Ortberg are manufacturing a story."

Too often when a pastor is accused of misconduct, the initial response includes denial, deflection, displays of bewilderment or anger, and demonization of the accuser. Typically, the allegations are met with a strong denial by the pastor, elders, or other leaders, followed quickly by an alternative narrative of "what really happened." These new narratives sow seeds of doubt about the veracity, stability, and motives of the accuser; seek to minimize the seriousness of the charges; suggest that innocent words or actions were misunderstood or misinterpreted; and often attempt to widen the locus of accusation to include not only the pastor, but also the elders or church board, the ministry, or the church itself—as if questioning the pastor's integrity or behavior was an attack on the entire church. It's also not uncommon for church leadership to offer assurances that the issue has already been investigated, addressed, and resolved internally. When I saw this pattern begin to emerge in the *Tribune*'s story about Willow Creek, my gut instinct told me to trust the *women* as the truth tellers.

"I hope the church doesn't come out swinging," I told Laura. "There's going to be huge fallout if they don't handle these allegations compassionately."

Well, they didn't respond compassionately, as I later detailed on my *Jesus Creed* blog:

> Willow Creek's leadership [made] . . . an egregiously
> unwise decision: it chose to narrate the allegations as lies,

the women as liars, and the witnesses to the women as colluders. Alongside that accusing narrative . . . [they] ran another narrative: Bill Hybels was innocent, the work of God at Willow Creek will continue, and we'll get through this. They called this difficult challenge a "season." This combined narrative of accusing-the-women and defending-Bill is both a narrative and a strategy.[5]

What happened in the aftermath of this initial counterpunch by Bill Hybels and the leadership of Willow Creek was widely well-examined by mainstream, online, and social media. Our purpose here is not to get sucked into the vortex of Willow, but to use this example as one of several illustrations of what can happen when a church's culture becomes toxic.

We begin with the unraveling of Willow Creek because this is a story that matters to our family: Laura and Mark, Scot and Kris. We attended Willow Creek for years, and Mark and Laura met in the young-adult ministry there. We know many, if not most, of the people who are directly involved. We deeply love Willow Creek, and we pray for a full reconciliation there.

However, this is far from being a book just about Willow Creek. Sadly, and unsurprisingly, we didn't have to look very far to find other examples of toxic and dysfunctional churches. Even as the Willow Creek story continued to unfold, Harvest Bible Chapel, another of Chicagoland's flagship churches, parted ways with its founding pastor, James MacDonald, when the board of elders determined that MacDonald was "biblically disqualified . . . from ministry" after decades of "insulting, belittling, and verbally bullying others . . . improperly exercising positional and spiritual authority over others to his own advantage . . . [and] extravagant spending utilizing church resources resulting in personal benefit" as part of "a substantial pattern of sinful behavior."[6]

And the problem is not isolated to Chicago megachurches. In the absence of a culture that *resists* abuse and promotes healing, safety, and spiritual growth, the heartbreaking truth is that churches of all shapes and sizes are susceptible to abuses of power, sexual abuse, and spiritual abuse.

Just in the past few years, we've seen allegations arise against Sovereign Grace Ministries and one of its founders, C. J. Mahaney, for their handling of abuse within SGM congregations.[7] We've seen former youth pastors such as Andy Savage and Wes Feltner resign from their churches because of allegations that they sexually abused young women who were part of their ministries.[8] We've seen megachurch pastor Mark Driscoll ousted from the church-planting network he helped found because of what the network's board considered "ungodly and disqualifying behavior."[9] We've seen allegations even against Southwestern Baptist Theological Seminary, which under the leadership of president Paige Patterson "had a custom and practice of ignoring female students' complaints of sexual harassment and stalking behavior by male student-employees," according to a legal complaint filed in the state of Texas.[10] And the ongoing story of alleged sexual abuse within the Roman Catholic Church has been headline news for decades.

But it's too easy to scapegoat the immediate perpetrator and ignore that these behaviors typically don't happen in a vacuum. Rather, they express the *culture* of an institution. The tragedy of these and far too many other stories is that, instead of focusing on the wounded, the victims, and the survivors of abuse, these organizations focused on themselves, on their leadership, on their own self-interest. They protected the guilty, hid from accountability, and silenced the wounded. And that only scratches the surface of the problem.

The impact is sobering: There is a loss of innocence and a

growing disillusionment for innumerable good people in whose lives the church plays a central role, people who viewed their pastor as an exemplary role model of how to be a Christian, how to be a godly husband, father, grandfather, pastor, leader, and movement creator. And this is true for many others who considered their church to be the epitome of success. Some people, when the curtain was pulled back on their church's leadership, discovered a level of duplicity and corruption that could not be believed—and therefore *would not* be believed. For so many others, there has also been a loss of trust—in pastors, elders, leaders of megachurch corporations, of churches in general, of anything having to do with Christianity. These are real people and real wounds that require healing.

A WORD TO THE WOUNDED
AND TO WOUNDED RESISTERS

If you are one of the church's wounded, you need to know that Jesus cares about you. He sees you, he knows what you have been through, and he can heal you from your pain.

If you're wondering, *How could God have let this happen?* there is a passage at the end of Matthew 9 that may speak to you. It's easy to overlook, tucked in between a series of ten stories in which Jesus uses his miraculous healing power to save, transform, rehabilitate, and restore wounded lives and the commissioning of his twelve disciples to take this ministry of healing and deliverance "to the lost sheep of the house of Israel."[11] In the middle of this transition, we find a beautiful verse:

> When [Jesus] saw the crowds, he had compassion on
> them, because they were harassed and helpless, like sheep
> without a shepherd.[12]

Notice how Matthew describes the crowds—as *harassed* and *helpless*. He also says they were "like sheep without a shepherd," which is how many people wounded by pastors and churches may feel. It was on those who had been ignored by the powerful leaders of Israel that Jesus focused his compassion, love, grace, and redemption.

But here's the part we don't want you to miss. Immediately after showing compassion for these desperate and hurting people, Jesus turns to his disciples and says, "The harvest is great, but the workers are few. So pray to the Lord who is in charge of the harvest; ask him to send more workers into his fields."[13] Because there are so many wounded, Jesus says, we need a host of wounded healers. In other words, if you are a disciple of Jesus, you have been commissioned—not only to see and hear and believe the wounded, but also to care for them, to bind up their wounds and heal their afflictions.

Our book is about wounded healers and wounded resisters: women and men who did the right thing, who told the truth, who suffered rejection, intimidation, and revictimization, but who persevered in telling the truth so the truth would be known.

This is a book about defending the redemptive value of the church while at the same time accepting the truth that broken and fallen people within the church—including pastors and other leaders—will sin, sometimes in shameful and damaging ways.

This is for the women, and others, who have brought allegations against trusted leaders and who grieve over their church's sick culture, and for countless other men and women, boys and girls who have told their story to no one outside the circle of family, trusted friends, and counselors. Though they may not have spoken publicly, they don't lack for courage or Christian character or goodness. For any number of reasons, they continue to be triggered in silence, suffer in silence, and try to heal in silence. But their prayers are heard by the God who heals, and he is the one who will ultimately establish justice.

Above all, this is a book of *hope*—about a better way, a way we're calling the Circle of *Tov** (from the Hebrew word for *good*), and what it takes to form a culture of *goodness* in our churches that will resist abuses of power, promote healing, and eradicate the toxic fallout that infects so many Christian organizations. Whatever else might be said, we need to learn how to keep these devastating events from repeating themselves in other churches and ministries. We need a map to get us from where we are today to where we ought to be as the body of Christ on earth.

The map we're offering is contained in the word *tov*. We will use this word throughout the book, and it is an essential part of the title. To begin to understand the breadth and depth of this little three-letter word, we can open our Bibles to the very first page, where it pops up seven times.

> Light is *tov*,
> land and sea are *tov*,
> plants are *tov*,
> day and night are *tov*,
> sea animals and birds are *tov*,
> land animals are *tov*.[14]

And then the seventh: "God saw all that he had made, and it was very *tov*."[15] So everything God created is *tov*. And when everything is spoken and accomplished, when all the intricate harmonies are formed, God's glory echoes through all creation: *tov me'od*. Very good! Very well done! Perfect! Harmony! What a

---

* *Tov* is pronounced with a long ō (rhymes with rove).

masterpiece! All these English terms, and more, are found in the word *tov*. In this book, we will focus on forming churches that God can look at and say, "Now that's *tov*!"

First, we will explore how church cultures are formed and sometimes *de*formed. In order to talk about goodness, we must examine some of the toxic church cultures that have made this book necessary. Next, we will discuss the symptoms and warning signs that are common to toxic cultures. Finally, we will explain how to create a culture of goodness that incorporates what we're calling the Circle of *Tov*.

* * *

As we begin, may we offer a simple prayer—that God will be gracious, that God will forgive, that God will heal, that God will restore people to himself and to one another, and that *tov* will abound in our churches.

PART 1

FORMING AND DEFORMING A CHURCH'S CULTURE

Never underestimate the power of the environment you work in to gradually transform who you are. When you choose to work at a certain company, you are turning yourself into the sort of person who works in that company. . . . Moreover, living life in a pragmatic, utilitarian manner turns you into a utilitarian pragmatist.

DAVID BROOKS, *THE SECOND MOUNTAIN*

There are good guys and bad guys, and the bad guys, using illegitimate methods, are trying to bring about an evil state of affairs. This can only be averted if the good guys mobilize their forces, recruit people from the sidelines (who are in danger of being seduced by the bad guys), and press forward to glorious victory.

ROGER C. SCHANK AND ROBERT P. ABELSON,
KNOWLEDGE AND MEMORY: THE REAL STORY

An organization or culture that perpetuates abuse will question the motives of those who ask questions, make the discussion of problems the problem, condemn those who condemn, silence those who break silence, and descend upon those who dissent.

WADE MULLEN

*The villainies of villains are evil;
they devise wicked devices
to ruin the poor with lying words,
even when the plea of the needy is right.*

ISAIAH 32:7, NRSV

1

EVERY CHURCH IS A CULTURE

CULTURE IS IMPORTANT. The culture in which we live teaches us how to behave and how to think. We learn what is right and wrong, good and bad, by living in a culture that defines these things. We learn our moral intuitions, beliefs, convictions—whatever term you want to use—in community, in relationship with others. Culture *socializes* us into what is considered proper behavior. For Christians, this is true in our churches as well as in society at large.

Think about what you believed was normal and right and good when you were a child. Now think of what you believed was normal and right and good after you became a Christian and as you grew as a follower of Jesus. Where did you learn your instincts? From the culture at home and from the culture within the church. For example, in the culture of the church where I (Scot) grew up, I learned it was wrong to go to movies, that any Bible other than the King James Version was not what God wanted, and that the faith of Methodists, Presbyterians, Episcopalians, and (especially) Roman Catholics was suspect.

Culture affects everyone. There is no un-enculturated person anywhere in the world. No one is unrelated, un-networked, un-embedded, un-enmeshed, or un-systemic. We're all shaped by our interactions with others, and that shaping becomes the culture in which we are all related, networked, embedded, enmeshed, and systemically connected.

Like any organization, every church is a distinct culture, formed and nurtured and perpetuated by the ongoing interaction of leaders and congregants. In addition, every church culture has a life of its own. However a church is organized—with a senior pastor, lead pastor, teaching pastor, rector, or priest, along with associates, curates, elders, deacons, directors, and ministry leaders—the leaders guide the organization *toward* a particular culture. But they're not the only ones who have a say in the matter. The congregation, too, is involved in shaping the culture of the church. So, though it is true that leaders lead and thus have a decisive and sometimes overriding voice in the formation of culture, it's more accurate to say that leaders and congregations form the church's culture *together*.

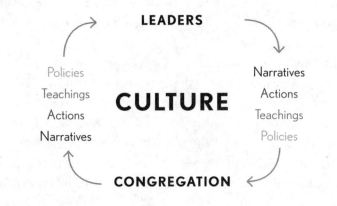

Think of it this way: Pastors and other leaders exercise a pre-liminary voice in forming and telling the church's *narrative, acting out* the Christian life for others to see, *teaching* the Christian faith and how it is lived, and articulating *policies.* They exercise formal authority and power to create and maintain the church's culture. Ideally, they do this in a good way. The congregation, both individually and collectively, embraces the culture but also begins to *reshape* the narrative, *act out* the Christian life for others to see, *reteach* the Christian faith, and *rearticulate* the policies. Thus, the congregation exercises its own authority and power to shape and maintain the culture. Over time, it is the interaction of the leaders and congregation, the congregation and leaders, that forms the culture of a church. In that sense, everyone in the church is "complicit" in whatever culture is formed, good or bad.

Not only does every church culture have a life of its own, but that life is *powerful, self-perpetuating,* and *always changing.* In other words, the culture created and nurtured by the pastor, church leaders, and congregation becomes a self-reinforcing agent of both *change* and *conformity*—forming and shaping, shaping and forming. As *New York Times* columnist David Brooks observes, culture acts upon us and makes us fit into it—like an invisible yet influential person working behind the scenes to keep us in line. In his book *The Second Mountain*, Brooks describes how culture is powerful enough to form us into its own image:

> Never underestimate the power of the environment you work in to gradually transform who you are. When you choose to work at a certain company, you are turning yourself into the sort of person who works in that company. . . .
>
> Moreover, living life in a pragmatic, utilitarian manner turns you into a utilitarian pragmatist. The "How do I succeed?" questions quickly eclipse the "Why am I doing this?" questions.[1]

What people experience in contact with your church—its services, its leaders, its people, its programs—defines your church's culture. If you look at the behaviors of the most industrious workers in a church, you will see the culture of that church in action. Those dutiful servants embody the *life* of the church. Thus, a church's culture is not incidental. Your church *is* its culture, and that culture *is* your church. Never underestimate the transformative power of culture. If you want to create a culture of goodness (*tov*), it is profoundly important to understand the type of culture your church has now.

Compassion will characterize a church's culture when the congregation and leaders consistently interact in compassionate ways, until a critical mass of compassion tips the balance in the direction of becoming a compassionate culture. When a church's culture is rooted in compassion, it creates an environment of safety, security, and openness.

Toxicity will take root in a church's culture when the

congregation and leaders interact in toxic and dysfunctional ways, until the balance tips in the direction of toxicity. When a church's culture becomes toxic, the challenge to resist becomes harder and harder. To resist a toxic culture—especially one that is famous for its ministries, its leaders, its impact—requires courage, hope, and perseverance. Never underestimate the power of culture.

The bad news and the good news about culture can be summed up in the same statement: A rooted culture is almost *irresistible*. If the reinforcing culture is toxic, it becomes systemically corrupted and corrupts the people within it. Like racism, sexism, political ideologies, and success-at-all-costs businesses, a corrupted culture drags everyone down with it. On the other hand, if the reinforcing culture is *redemptive* and *healing* and *good* (*tov*), it becomes systemically good. A *tov* church culture will instinctively heal, redeem, and restore.

David Brooks makes a powerful statement about the incremental habits and practices that transform us over time:

> When people make generosity part of their daily routine, they refashion who they are. The interesting thing about your personality, your essence, is that it is not more or less permanent like your leg bone. Your essence is changeable, like your mind. Every action you take, every thought you have, changes you, even if just a little, making you a little more elevated or a little more degraded. If you do a series of good deeds, the habit of other-centeredness becomes gradually engraved into your life. It becomes easier to do good deeds down the line. If you lie or behave callously or cruelly toward someone, your personality degrades, and it is easier for you to do something even worse later on.[2]

Organizations function in the same way as individuals; that is, their habits form their personality. We've all been in churches and "felt the vibe." We've been in churches that seem like rigorous military organizations; in others we've sensed chaos. Still other churches feel like an art gallery, a concert venue, a stage production, or a grand show. In some churches, you get the sense that everyone has gathered to hear (and even adore) the preacher or speaker, and everything else they do is merely to round out the service. In other churches, the sermon, or homily, is part of a progression leading up to the celebration of Communion or the Eucharist. In the past two decades, my wife, Kris, and I (Scot) have been in hundreds of churches. Often, when we reflect on a church we've visited, Kris will say something like this: "If we lived in that city, we'd want to be a part of that church."

I (Laura) attended a church recently whose culture might best be described as Celebrity Central. All the people on stage seemed to be adored by the people sitting in the seats. One of the first things that happened during the service was recognition for the senior pastor's good and faithful work. This recognition was immediately followed by a standing ovation for the senior pastor.

As the service progressed, I was struck by the number of times the congregation applauded the people on stage. Without exaggeration, it was at least ten times. What occurred to me was that whenever something good was said about the church, the people applauded—which became, in essence, *self*-applause. This church's laudatory culture stood in stark contrast to the culture in the church where I normally worship, where applause of any kind is exceedingly rare. I'm not saying one is right or better, but the cultures are certainly different.

We form church cultures, but we are simultaneously formed *by* the cultures we've helped to form. It's like marriage. Marry someone, and before long you and your spouse will shape each other.

Out of that mutual shaping and forming grows a culture of love. That culture of love and concern and commitment begins to shape you and your spouse—and on and on it goes. This is one dimension of what the Bible means by "the two become one."

Unfortunately, the same process applies to a bad marriage, except you and your partner are now shaping each other in negative ways. Instead of forming a culture of love, some couples form a toxic culture of tension, criticism, avoidance, poor communication, and passive-aggressive behavior.

Either way, whenever people get together, forming a culture is inevitable. And that culture inevitably shapes everyone in the culture.

Culture speaks to the underlying tenor of relationships within the church, as well. It is seen in the values and priorities that govern day-to-day life. A church culture isn't formed by someone launching a program—for compassion or justice or kindness or goodness—however noble the cause may be. Volunteerism does not make a culture. Programs may enlist volunteers, who may be changed by such programs, but programs alone do not establish a culture. Neither do the persuasive powers of a program leader. Culture formation requires time; it requires relationships that evolve over time, it requires mutual interaction over time.

Sometimes we want change because we see something amiss in our church, so we launch a program. Let's say the congregation is mostly white and suddenly realizes they have ignored the Latin American culture in their community. Launching a program that invests in or "reaches out" to such a culture will not change the culture in the church. It may initiate change, but developing an integrated church requires an ongoing commitment and lots of time. It requires relationships, lengthy conversations, adjustments and changes. We could go on, but the point is obvious: Cultures form over time, and it takes time to shift a culture.

Andy Crouch, author of *Culture Making*, warns us against thinking that culture is merely synonymous with *worldview*—how we understand, analyze, and think about life. He prefers to define culture as "what human beings *make* of the world,"[3] both in the sense of how we *perceive* the world and what we *do* with it—our practices and habits and the things we make. This definition dovetails nicely with the idea we've been discussing here of the mutual forming and shaping aspects of culture as an ever-changing, powerful, and self-perpetuating *agent* in our lives. Crouch goes on to say, "The language of worldview tends to imply . . . that we can *think* our way into new ways of behaving. But that is not how culture works. Culture helps us *behave* ourselves into new ways of thinking."[4] In other words, through our *actions*, culture shapes our *thinking*. A good (*tov*) culture teaches us to behave with goodness, and good behavior shapes our thoughts toward goodness. What Crouch is suggesting, then, is that a church culture is an agent that actively influences us.

Here is an example recounted by a church leader of how a toxic culture can overcome initial resistance, create a rationalization, and eventually change a person's behavior.

> While working for a church in a large metropolitan area . . . I routinely saw others [on staff] treated meanly and harshly by the lead minister and others in his good graces. . . . Staff members were often pitted against another, creating jealousy and unhealthy competition instead of unity, teamwork and brotherhood. It was a way to keep everybody off-balance, insecure and striving to avoid getting on the lead minister's "bad list." People were mostly motivated out of fear. . . .
>
> What did I do when I initially saw abuse on the staff?

- I was shocked.
- I was glad it wasn't directed against me.
- I rationalized that this ridiculous behavior must be what "real discipleship" is all about. . . .
- I trusted the leadership that this type of training was what it took to become an effective minister. . . .
- I thought these people somehow deserved this mistreatment. . . .
- I was afraid that if I objected, I would be next.

Worse, I started to imitate this behavior. . . .

Once, our house church group was playing volleyball at an apartment complex. I let one of the guys borrow my sunglasses. After it got dark, he had put them down somewhere and couldn't find them anymore. He came and told me, and though it was pitch dark out and late on a weeknight, I harshly told him, "Go find them."

Another time, our group had a picnic. One of the young women in the group playfully tossed some ice down my back, and I took it as evidence that she wasn't giving me the respect I was due as the leader. So I scolded and belittled her in front of everybody. . . .

I'm not blaming others for what I did, but the culture of abuse just has a way of expanding. I learned it, I practiced it, and then I passed it on to others.[5]

I learned it, I practiced it, and then I passed it on to others. Culture is a powerful formative agent. When the culture is toxic, as in the example above, abusive habits are reinforced and repeated.

Thinking about the importance and impact of culture is nothing new. The Bible is full of examples, both good and bad. The Bible also adds an element that is vital to our understanding of cultural formation; namely that it emerges from the *character* of the people who shape the culture.

JESUS, CHARACTER, AND CULTURE

As we've seen in one ministry meltdown after another, character plays an indispensable role in forming, preserving, and undergirding a church's culture. A lack of character in leadership can destroy decades of hard work, vision, and growth—in the blink of an eye.

Jesus taught about the centrality of character, and how to discern good character from bad:

> A tree is identified by its fruit. If a tree is good, its fruit will be good. If a tree is bad, its fruit will be bad.[6]

Another word about bad character:

> You brood of snakes! How could evil men like you speak what is good and right? For whatever is in your heart determines what you say.[7]

And a corresponding word about good character:

> A good person produces good things from the treasury of a good heart, and an evil person produces evil things from the treasury of an evil heart.[8]

Character works from the inside out: A good heart produces good things, but an evil heart produces evil.

The apostle Paul also zeroes in on character, though he uses the metaphor of *flesh* and *spirit* instead of trees and fruit. In Galatians 5:19-23, he contrasts the "acts of the flesh" and the "fruit of the

Spirit."[9] It is worth noting that both flesh and spirit express the core of one's character.

Toxic, flesh-driven cultures breed a lust for power, success, celebrity, control through fear, an emphasis on authority, and demands for loyalty. These values may not be explicitly stated, or even outwardly recognized, but as they fester in the heart of a leader, they can't help but bear bitter fruit, damaging the culture of the church and seeking to destroy anyone who gets in the way.

A Spirit-formed, Christlike culture, on the other hand, nurtures truth, offers healing for the wounded, seeks opportunities to show redemptive grace and love, focuses on serving others (rather than on being served), and looks for ways to establish justice in the daily paths of life. A Christlike church culture always has its eyes on people because the mission of the church is all about God's redemptive love for people.

This book is about the characteristics or habits of churches that form a Christlike culture, or what we will later develop as a culture of *goodness* or *tov*. But before we can turn our focus to how to create a goodness culture, we must first look at the dangers of a culture that has become toxic. Part of our purpose in writing is to help churches identify the warning signs of toxicity. It is to this regrettable but necessary task that we now turn.

EARLY WARNING SIGNS OF A TOXIC CULTURE

WHEN YOU CONSIDER THAT JESUS intended to establish a church that was on a mission "to proclaim good news to the poor . . . and recovery of sight for the blind, to set the oppressed free, to proclaim the year of the Lord's favor,"[1] it is tragically ironic that church leadership, formed as it is by the character of the leaders, can do so much harm. In this chapter, we want to draw attention to two early warning signs of a toxic culture: *narcissism* and *power through fear*.

1. NARCISSISM

For some reason, church leadership at times seems to attract unempathetic, selfish narcissists. Whether narcissists simply find their way to the top (which must be somewhat true) or the top of the leadership tower attracts narcissists (which also must be somewhat true), far too many churches have narcissists in leadership. And they are predominately male.[2]

If we are to have any hope of developing a goodness (*tov*) culture in our churches, these narcissistic, unempathetic leaders must be resisted or replaced. To do that, we must understand how toxic, narcissistic cultures develop in the first place.

Even as second graders, some of my (Laura's) students are fascinated with Greek and Roman mythology. Perhaps because superheroes have become so popular in contemporary culture, tales of mythological gods and goddesses have captured their attention. My reading groups sometimes discuss word origins to assist with vocabulary development, so we look at connections such as Odysseus and *odyssey*, Chronos and *chronology*, the Muses and *musical*, and Narcissus and *narcissism*. I've read the story of Narcissus to my students; and if you ask them, they will tell you about the impossibly handsome god who fell in love with his own image. The Greek and Roman versions of the myth vary a bit, but the story line is the same: Narcissus walks by a pond or lake one day, sees his own image reflected in the water, and becomes entranced. But because it is only an image, he cannot obtain the object of his affection. So he dies, either from sorrow (in the Greek version) or suicide (in the Roman version).

"What does this myth teach us?" I ask my students. "What can you apply to your own life?"

Inevitably, someone will answer, "Well, he should have quit staring at himself" or "He really stared at himself for way too long."

As we discuss *why* Narcissus was staring at himself, I guide them toward a definition of narcissism like this one: "Narcissists are people who care only about themselves—what they look like and what other people think about them." My students are honest and discerning in their responses: "He shouldn't do that," they say.

It's easy to *label* someone a narcissist and be done with it. But

what if narcissism is actually *dangerous*? We need a better understanding of the personality type because (sorry to say) narcissists
are far too prevalent in our churches. We must develop the ability
to spot them before they can do harm.

The Mayo Clinic offers a helpful definition:

> Narcissistic personality disorder . . . is a mental
> condition in which people have an inflated sense of their
> own importance, a deep need for excessive attention
> and admiration, troubled relationships, and a lack of
> empathy for others. But behind this mask of extreme
> confidence lies a fragile self-esteem that's vulnerable to
> the slightest criticism.[3]

Though a narcissist may possess what is commonly known
as a "strong personality," that perceived strength often disguises
insecurity and a deep need to feel superior and successful. The
selfish drive for importance compels narcissistic pastors to sur-
round themselves with admirers. They will break relationship
with people who don't give them the esteem and honor they
desire. Narcissists often gravitate toward enablers, who will pave
their way to power—or at least not stand in the way. The opera-
tive term that describes these enablers is *sycophants*—people who
fawn over someone in a position of power and influence in order
to gain power and influence of their own. Some pastors nurture
sycophants, and before long the elder board or deacon board is
populated with apple-polishers who are malleable to the pastor's
will and often unwilling to stand up to the pastor with solid—and
necessary—biblical oversight.

Plutarch, the Roman philosopher and essayist, wrote a treatise
titled *How to Tell a Flatterer from a Friend* that hits the nail on the
head about leaders and empire builders. One needs only the title

of the essay to get the whole point: The last thing a powerful man or woman needs is a flatterer whispering sweet affirmations all day long, and the first thing he or she needs is a friend who will speak frankly. "Wounds from a sincere friend are better than many kisses from an enemy," the Bible says.[4] Friends don't let friends become narcissists.

So how do narcissists end up leading churches? Do churches give their pastors too much power, tempting them to display narcissistic qualities? Or do narcissists ambitiously seek to acquire more power in a church? The answer is probably *both*. Either way, one of the most significant problems in churches today is the grasping for power of narcissistic pastors and leaders.

It is common for a narcissist to want his church to be seen as the *best*, the *biggest*, and the *most influential* because he believes the glory accrues to him as the leader. Praising a narcissist's church is the same as praising the pastor himself. It follows, then, that anyone who dares to criticize a narcissistic pastor will be attacked by the narcissist for threatening the status of "the best church ever" and the pastor's own self-importance.

Because the narcissist's self-image and the church's reputation are so deeply intertwined, rage is a common response to criticism, whether the criticism is direct or merely perceived. Sometimes the rage is kept under wraps, through seething or brooding or behind-the-scenes passive-aggressive actions; but you can be certain that anger is brewing in the heart of a criticized narcissist.

Repeatedly, in the course of our study, we heard or read stories about pastors and their extreme sensitivity to criticism (or what they perceived as criticism). Here's a revealing example from the *Willow Creek Governance Review* report:

> Historically, annual performance reviews had been
> a painful process for the elders because of the Senior

wounding power. When a leader manifests the power hatchet, a culture is formed that adjusts to the blade of fear. Power and fear are close companions. Combine this with narcissism, and a toxic culture is sure to form.

Perhaps the best explanation for why two of Chicagoland's most well-known churches were able to spin so far out of control was that a culture of fear had taken over in both. According to more than one of our sources, the phrase "fear of Bill" was common at Willow Creek, and an independent investigation confirmed it.[9] Elders and staff found it painful to confront Bill Hybels and would avoid questioning him for fear of his harsh reactions.[10]

At Harvest Bible Chapel, according to a report by Julie Roys in *World* magazine, "former elders, staff, and members . . . said Harvest has fostered an abusive and fear-based culture where those who question leadership are punished."[11] Two former elders at Harvest were formally excommunicated by the church and demonized in a video explaining the decision to the congregation, after they persisted in questioning decisions made by the board. One board member went so far as to say that "publicizing viewpoints rejected by the elder majority for any reason is satanic to the core."[12]

When other church leaders become complicit in a pastor's abuse of power, it casts a chilling shadow on the rest of the church and people become reluctant to speak up. Indeed, Gordon Zwirkoski, an original director at Harvest, said that James MacDonald nurtured "a spirit of fear in the staff, almost like a dread."[13] Moreover, MacDonald could only be removed as pastor "by a unanimous vote of the full elder board and the executive committee"—of which MacDonald himself was a member.[14]

Once a culture of fear forms within a church, there's almost no turning back. As a historian of ancient Greece said in summarizing one of its most powerful leaders, "Tyranny . . . was a delightful place, but there was no way out of it."[15] This is why we must retrain ourselves to think biblically and live in a different narrative; that is, in a story of goodness. Old Testament scholar Ellen Davis states it perfectly: "The sages of Israel teach that those who would be wise must aim, not at power, but at goodness."[16] Power and goodness are not close buddies.

As Ronald Enroth, an expert on power-based church leaders, describes it, an abusive, fear-based church culture emerges with power-mongering leaders:

> *Ruler* is the right term to describe the kind of people in authoritarian leadership roles. . . . They are spiritual tyrants who take unholy pleasure in requiring obedience and subordination of their followers. It is important to recognize that leadership depends on followership, and from a truly Christian perspective, that means cooperation *with* the leader rather than domination and control *by* the leader. The source of legitimate Christian leadership therefore lies in *entrusted authority*.
>
> The spiritual autocrat, the religious dictator, attempts to compel subordination; the true Christian leader can legitimately only elicit followership.[17]

More needs to be said about abuses of power because power-and-fear-based church cultures are on the rise. I (Scot) have seen on the faces of many (mainly women) a witness to the harsh reality and intense pain caused by such pastors. We need to dig a little deeper, therefore, into the dynamics of a power-and-fear-based culture, because once it becomes established, it's very difficult to uproot.

Recent research has uncovered some alarming evidence of the effects that power has on the human brain. For example:

Subjects under the influence of power . . . acted as if they had suffered traumatic brain injury—becoming more impulsive, less risk-aware, and, crucially, less adept at seeing things from other people's point of view.

Sukhvinder Obhi, a neuroscientist at McMaster University, in Ontario, recently described something similar. . . . When he put the heads of the powerful and the not-so-powerful under a transcranial-magnetic-stimulation machine, he found that power, in fact, impairs a specific neural process, "mirroring," that may be a cornerstone of empathy. Which gives a neurological basis to what [Dacher] Keltner has termed the "power paradox": Once we have power, we lose some of the capacities we needed to gain it in the first place.[18]

If we can't mirror or mimic, we lose our capacity to empathize with others. Alongside this empathy deficit in powerful people is what behavioral scientists David Owen and Jonathan Davidson identify as *hubris syndrome*. "Hubris syndrome is a disorder of the possession of power, particularly power which has been associated with overwhelming success, held for a period of years and with minimal constraint on the leader."[19] Symptoms include "a disproportionate concern with image and presentation; . . . contempt for the advice or criticism of others; exaggerated self-belief . . . in what they personally can achieve; . . . loss of contact with reality; . . . restlessness, recklessness and impulsiveness."[20]

When leaders acquire power, power itself becomes an agent that may reduce the leader's capacity for empathy and compassion, especially toward those who are powerless (like women, in many churches). Such a self-centered hubris may cause the personal character of the power-shaped pastor to lose contact with the very essence of Christianity. We will look more at this later.

To summarize the kind of culture that forms when narcissists gain power and use fear to keep people in line, we have identified eight indicators that anyone can use to evaluate their own church's culture.

EIGHT PHASES OF A POWER-THROUGH-FEAR CULTURE

There can be no escaping the reality that many Christians, some of them abused in awful ways, are scared to death to talk about what they've seen or heard at church. They've lived in a culture of fear, and fear has driven them to silence. How does a fear culture develop? We believe there are eight phases in the formation of a power-through-fear culture.

1. It begins when *power and authority are vested in an individual*—most often a *pastor* (but not always) and most often a *man* (but not always)—and it can spread to other leaders and influencers in the congregation. This power emerges from a pastor's position, giftedness, persuasiveness, and perceived success. Other leaders, some of whom are sycophants riding coattails on a narcissist's insatiable desire for glory, affirm that power and thus enhance it. Glory starts to be passed around: The pastor affirms an elder, and that elder affirms another elder, who affirms someone in the congregation. Before long, the pastor is surrounded by a circle of beholden power-and-glory-makers.

2. *The pastor's approval becomes the gold standard.* Those whom the pastor approves are approved. Churches that develop a fear culture almost always develop a perceived connection between the pastor's power and God's approval. It's a sickness, a contagious disease, and it can be deadly to the spiritual health of the congregation.

A study by Mark Allan Powell, a Lutheran seminary professor, showed "how differently the pastor and the congregation interpret

Scripture."[21] In his book titled *What Do They Hear?*, Powell makes an interesting observation: When laypeople read the Gospels, they identify with the disciples or with the marginalized people mentioned in the stories. When pastors read the same Gospel stories, they identify with Jesus. Why? Perhaps because when pastors preach stories from God's Word, they stand in as the mouthpiece of God. Before long, they come to identify more with Jesus than with those in need of grace. This goes a long way toward explaining what we're discussing here: Powerful pastors become associated too easily with God in the minds of the congregation. Which is why their approval matters. Many people in churches seem to think, *If Pastor approves of me, then God must approve of me.* And some pastors may want them thinking that way.

3. *Those approved by the power pastor gain "status enhancement."* When members of a congregation are affirmed and approved by the pastor—seen as a God-anointed messenger, a religious authority who speaks for God—their status within the church becomes "insider," "significant," and yes, for many, "powerful." Their self-esteem goes up, they feel cool and "in," and they become somewhat intoxicated with their newfound status.

I (Scot) have had many conversations over the years with young leaders who had recently acquired a significant position at a megachurch. Though all were gifted (and thus well deserving of their new calling), what was obvious was that they were basking in their new status in ways beyond their own self-awareness. There's nothing wrong with enjoying a new job or a promotion within one's church. But my concern, and what I find potentially dangerous, is the evident status enhancement these young leaders felt from gaining the approval of a power pastor.

Here's an example: At a conference, I met a young woman who worked at a megachurch. She told me that every time she drives onto the church campus, she pinches herself to see if it's real. And then she said, "It makes me feel really important to work here." That's status enhancement.

4. *Power cuts with both sides of the blade.* Along with the power of approval and the ability to confer status enhancement comes the other side of the knife: the power of *disapproval* and "status degradation." Power leaders carry the two-edged sword conspicuously. In subtle and not-so-subtle ways, they make it known that they can use it whenever they want (and almost no one can do anything about it).

5. *The power-shaping culture transitions into a fear-shaped culture.* People who derive their status from the pastor's approval live in constant fear of being disapproved at any moment. The church may well preach God's unconditional love, but a fear-shaped culture is all about conditional approval. In some fear cultures, the power pastor, leaders, and "approval group" control the narrative and provide enough positive feedback for people to at least think they know where they stand. But the blade of reversal is ever-present, and in some churches is constantly on display.

I (Laura) believe I experienced the disapproval phase firsthand at Willow Creek. I lost friendships—including one that was decades long—over what I said on social media and for refusing to apologize for my criticism of the church's handling of events. I got the back side of the blade because my words did not match the conditions required for approval. Almost every victim, outspoken advocate, and resister with whom I've connected has spoken of lost relationships. The women who brought forth the first allegations, and those who supported them, endured far worse. Willow Creek's approval group closed ranks and showed us all the razor-sharp blade.

6. *Judgments and decisions are rendered behind a wall of secrecy.* In a power-through-fear culture, the powerful pastor and his close associates decide what information will be disseminated and what will be held back. The privilege of knowing what is going on, one

quickly learns, is for insiders' eyes and ears only. People resign and leave with no explanation, often "called to a new ministry," and only the insiders know why. This form of secrecy induces fear in other staff members to stay in line. When someone leaves, he or she is encouraged to "end well," which means "don't talk." Secrecy remains.

7. *Behind the wall of secrecy lurks a perpetual fear of status degradation.* Along with the fear of being demoted, moved from the inside circle to the outer edges, or shown the door, there is also a fear of being shamed by having one's status publicly revoked. Shame is the experience of being humiliated. All of these intense human experiences—status degradation, demotion, shame, and humiliation—are inevitable in a fear culture, and their presence is a warning that a fear culture exists.

Bill Hybels, in his 2008 book *Axiom*, wrote a chapter called "Develop a Mole System," in which he describes "communication conduits" he established at Willow Creek:

> I strike an intentional arrangement wherein they [the moles] provide me regular feedback on weekend services or conference sessions or how we are really doing in a department we have recently reorganized. . . . With all these folks—whether they know they're operating as my "moles" or not—the lines of communication are wide open.[22]

At first, this approach may seem like a decent one. Hybels describes responsible leadership and the importance of understanding an organization. But then he says:

> My direct reports need to know that I have other sources than the ones sitting right in front of me week in and week out. If they're working hard and keeping me informed along the way, then the conversations I have

[with moles] . . . should be of no concern. And if they have been painting a rosier picture than the truth, I don't mind their knowing that I'm likely to find that out over time.[23]

What does this sound like? Fear induction. "I don't mind their knowing that I'm likely to find out" is a classic statement of the power-through-fear mindset. Likewise, having a strategically devised "mole system." The very use of the word *mole* conjures images of a spy or undercover agent. What is the purpose of a mole? To secretly report information. Bill Hybels used information he gained from these "communication conduits" to instill fear, and the moles were not unaware of the power he had over them if they failed. One person told us, "Bill had moles all over the church building. I'd get calls immediately from Bill about something that went wrong in a service or meeting. Bill hadn't been there, but someone secretly told him." This is power-based, fear-inducing behavior.

8. The last phase of a power-based and fear-inducing culture is—no surprise—*removal from the circle entirely*. Banishment is the ultimate form of the power pastor's disapproval. It is experienced as total rejection, and often feels like disapproval by God himself. Once removed from the circle, people who have lived in a fear-inducing culture can lose their faith; more often, they need some form of mental health therapy. It takes years for some people to trust pastors and leaders again, and many develop a keen eye for the signs of a fear culture. Jill Monaco, a former executive assistant at Harvest Bible Chapel, wrote about her mental health after leaving the inner world of that megachurch:

I'll be honest . . . detoxing from fear is hard. After leaving HBC, I had a crippling fear of making mistakes or wrong decisions. Fear ran the show and controlled so many of my decisions. I'd sacrifice what was good for me to keep the peace. . . . There should be no fear of failure, fear of man, fear of authority, fear of independence, fear of consequences for speaking truth, fear of gossip, etc. in healthy organizations.[24]

Seeing fear used to control and silence people grieves us. This is as far from the *tov* way of Jesus as one can get.

What can you do if you begin to recognize the warning signs of a toxic church culture? Do you speak up? How do you speak up? What happens if you speak up? We turn to that next.

HOW TOXIC CULTURES RESPOND TO CRITICISM

WHEN AN ALLEGATION ARISES against a pastor, a leader, or a volunteer within a church, what the pastor or leadership does *first* will reveal the culture of the church—whether it is toxic or *tov*. If the response is *confession* and *repentance*, or *a commitment to finding the truth* if all the facts are not yet known, that church probably has a healthy, *tov* culture. On the other hand, if the pastor's first instinct is denial, some form of story or narrative about "what really happened," or a defensive posture against "those who would attack our church or ministry," there are toxic elements at work within that church's culture.

When the *Chicago Tribune* published its initial exposé of Willow Creek Community Church, detailing some of the early allegations against Bill Hybels, he sought to control the narrative by confidently, even vehemently, denying the accusations, both to the reporters from the *Tribune* and to the Willow Creek congregation. At a hastily called congregational "family meeting," he tried to reframe the story as a personal vendetta by several former colleagues and staff members:

> The lies you read about in the *Tribune* article are the tools this group is using to try to keep me from ending my tenure here at Willow with my reputation intact. . . . Many of these alleged incidents purportedly took place more than [20] years ago. The fact that they have been dredged up now and assembled in a calculated way demonstrates the determination of this group to do as much damage as they possibly can.[1]

The tendency of leaders in a toxic culture to deny, deny, deny in the face of allegations can also be seen in an article about Paige Patterson, former president of Southwestern Baptist Theological Seminary, who was ousted in 2019.

> Former Southern Baptist statesman Paige Patterson claimed a religious liberty defense, while **denying** the bulk of allegations in a lawsuit over his handling of sex abuse claims, in an answer filed Aug. 26 in federal court.
>
> Patterson . . . **denied** that Southwestern Baptist Theological Seminary in Fort Worth, Texas, was an unsafe place for women when he served as president there from 2003 until his termination last year at age 76.
>
> He also **disputed** accounts of a private meeting with a former female student . . . while at the same time claiming any information shared in the conversation is protected

by the Free Exercise Clause of the First Amendment to the U.S. Constitution.

In a lawsuit filed in May in U.S. District Court in Sherman, Texas, an Alabama woman . . . claimed she was stalked and later sexually assaulted multiple times by a male student employed on campus as a plumber.

She said Patterson **refused** to believe her stories until he had a chance to—in his own words—"break her down." She said in an August 2015 meeting also attended by her mother, Patterson **defended** the decision to enroll an alleged sexual predator, **grilled her** with questions about whether their sex was consensual and **told her** rape might in the long run be a "good thing" because the right man to be her husband would not care if she is a virgin.

Patterson gave a **blanket denial** to those allegations, claiming that any harm done to the woman resulted from actions of someone other than him. Trying to hold him liable for conduct delegated to others under the governing documents of a religious body like a seminary, he said, would violate the First Amendment. . . .

In his legal response, Patterson **disputed** characterization of his behavior as "extreme and outrageous." He also **denied** sharing false information about [the woman] for purposes of distribution.[2]

Speaking at a Southern Baptist Convention conference on sexual abuse in the church, Boz Tchividjian, founder and former head of Godly Response to Abuse in the Christian Environment (GRACE), told the attendees, "The system of this denomination is broken."[3]

FINDING AND TELLING THE TRUTH

In a healthy, *tov* culture, leaders will avoid denial and spin, in favor of finding and telling the truth—even when the truth is painful. Jim Van Yperen, founder and president of Metanoia Ministries, whose mission is to "discover and embrace reconciliation as a way of life," recommends a seven-step process "for public communication about sexual sin in the church (whether it is a sinner's public confession or leadership making a public statement)."[4] Those steps include the following:

1. Speak God's Word—that is, "use the words God would use to describe sin."
2. Be specific and succinct, honest and direct.
3. Take unconditional and comprehensive responsibility.
4. Express genuine remorse, and humbly ask forgiveness.
5. Submit to change.
6. Make appropriate restitution.
7. Seek full reconciliation—with an important caveat: "The goal of reconciliation is to restore a sinner to fellowship, not a leader to power."[5]

In our research, we learned of a compassionate, just, and truthful response to accusations of abuse at a Presbyterian church in Lexington, Kentucky. The church's senior minister, Robert Cunningham, responded with such goodness and kindness and truth that I (Laura) was moved to tears reading his posts about his church's past and hopes for the future. On the day I reread his story, Robert Cunningham fittingly tweeted, "Neither truth nor love are ever convenient. Choose them anyway."

In November 2017, Cunningham tweeted the following during the rise of the #MeToo movement:

I say let the stories come. Let them all come out. . . . Let
every attempt to deflect or defend come to an end, and let
us instead listen and learn from the courage of the abused.
They are our prophets now, with voices that will no longer
allow us to hide or ignore the epidemic. . . . Indeed, the
overdue purge has begun, and may it not relent until every
hidden darkness faces the light of justice.[6]

Then, in June 2018, revealing his courage and compassion and
commitment to truth, he reposted the words on his church website with this addition:

I still believe that. Let it all come out. Let the purge
continue undaunted. Even when it is my own church's
past that needs purging.[7]

Cunningham then revealed the truth about Brad Waller, a
former Tates Creek pastor who directed the church's youth and
college ministries between 1995 and 2006. Waller was guilty of
"abuse of power against minors and young men under his care."[8]
One victim described a creepy, sexualized foot fetish incident with
Waller at an off-campus event for youth:

I remember sleeping in the tent and waking up to
something touching my feet. And as I woke up and
looked down, it was Brad, Pastor Brad. And he had his
face touching my feet. . . . I don't even remember him
being in the tent to start with.[9]

Waller eventually confessed to sinful patterns of abuse, stat-
ing his advances never went beyond foot-touching, but they were

sexualized.[10] Upon learning of Waller's advances toward young men, Cunningham immediately notified his congregation. He said, "We followed up with every name given to us, and through that process other acts of abuse were uncovered as well."[11]

> To summarize as clearly as possible: it has come to our attention that Brad Waller sexually abused boys and men under his care as a pastor of TCPC. While all of this misconduct took place over a decade ago, our church leadership is nevertheless committed to handling this horrific news with utmost sincerity, urgency, and transparency, which is why we have chosen to release this forthright statement.[12]

Cunningham learned of the abuse and responded by notifying pastors, elders, and the congregation, called a congregational meeting to share information and field questions, reported the abuse to police—who declined to investigate further—and hired an outside party to complete a thorough investigation.

> In this scenario, we are relinquishing control over the investigation and inviting any and all findings and corrections. . . . This will be an institutionally vulnerable process. Essentially, we are inviting an independent sexual abuse audit of our church, but we want everyone to know that TCPC wants to hide nothing. *That is not to say that mistakes were not made, only that if they were made, we don't want to hide them.* Instead, we want the opportunity to apologize and repent in any way we need to. Also, we want to be better equipped—both in policies and training—to make every effort to prevent this from

happening again at TCPC. Therefore, we welcome this investigation, along with its findings and applications.[13]

Cunningham apologized publicly and specifically to Waller's victims, the Tates Creek congregation, and the entire community of Lexington. When GRACE completed its investigation, Cunningham released the report, which is still posted on the church's website.[14]

What is remarkable here is that Robert Cunningham was not on staff at Tates Creek when these abusive events happened. And yet he was determined to try to make things right, to be as transparent as possible, to seek healing for all the victims. He felt an obligation to the church and to the victims to do the right thing, even though these events were long in the past. He apologized for the sin of a *former* pastor.

In our terms, Tates Creek has a *tov* culture. Therefore, goodness was shown to its people, and goodness came out of an otherwise toxic situation.

SPINNING MATTHEW 18

Another method that leaders in a toxic church culture sometimes use to control the narrative is to attack the *way* in which critical feedback or allegations of wrongdoing are brought to light. At Willow Creek, for example, the women and supporters who alleged inappropriate behavior by Bill Hybels were told they should have "followed Matthew 18" and talked to Bill privately first. This appeal to Scripture sounds right initially. Following the Bible is a good thing—except when "following the Bible" is actually *not* following the Bible. Here is the text of Matthew 18:15-17 (NRSV), along with some brief commentary:

> If another member of the church sins against you, go and
> point out the fault when the two of you are alone.[15]

Sometimes this kind of conversation works:

> If the member listens to you, you have regained that one.

Sometimes it doesn't work. There are no statistics on this, but some
people will never admit to doing anything wrong. They might
make excuses or try to cast blame somewhere else. They may try
to minimize or trivialize the other person's concern. They might
fake their way through an apology while plotting revenge. Or they
may flat-out deny everything. When such refusal happens, Jesus
said, try again, but take someone else with you as a witness:

> But if you are not listened to, take one or two others along
> with you, so that every word may be confirmed by the
> evidence of two or three witnesses.

If this doesn't work, the consequences become more serious:

> If the member refuses to listen to them, tell it to the
> church.

The goal of all these steps is to bring about repentance and restoration. But if telling the church doesn't work, the person must be
separated from the congregation. This has often been understood
to refer to excommunication:

> If the offender refuses to listen even to the church, let
> such a one be to you as a Gentile and a tax collector.

It's one thing to set this procedure in motion when someone has said something ugly about another person or has wrongly taken credit for something. But when a woman or a child who has been sexually abused is required to meet one-on-one with the perpetrator, it becomes morally inexcusable and psychologically violent to insist upon legalistically following Matthew 18. Such an approach becomes a cynical dodge and is almost always designed to protect the leader or the church. Yet it happens far too often.

At Willow Creek, "following Matthew 18" was trumpeted loudly by leaders who sought to protect the reputation of the institution rather than showing concern for the victims.[16] "We are deeply saddened by the way this has all played out in the media recently," the head of the Willow Creek elder board said on April 10, 2018, "and we're committed to moving forward in a biblical manner."[17] The obvious inference was that the women and their supporters, in going public, had taken an approach that was *not* biblical.

(It was not reported at the time, but according to Vonda Dyer, she and others *had* followed the model of Matthew 18 and *had* gone to Bill Hybels one-on-one. In Vonda's case, she said she confronted Hybels the morning after he kissed her in a hotel room in Sweden in 1998, telling him not to pursue her again or she would report his behavior. And then again, in 2000, when Vonda observed what she described as "a sexual energy" in Hybels when he was around five specific women at the church, including Nancy Beach and Nancy Ortberg, she said she went to his office and told him, "You need to knock it off." Not denying his flirtatious behavior, Hybels simply responded, "Understood.")[18]

A similar appeal to Matthew 18 was made by Wes Feltner, who was accused of carrying on secret relationships—one of them sexual—with two teenage female students in 2002 while serving as their youth pastor at First Southern Baptist Church in Evansville, Indiana. After years of suppressed silence (more on that later), the two women went public with their stories. In response, Feltner took issue not with the allegations but with *how* the abuse came to light:

> The Bible directs God's people to take their grievances first to the person accused and, if that person won't listen, to try again and bring a witness; and if the person still won't listen, then to take it to the church (Matthew 18:15-17). The group circulating these allegations did not bring them to me, rather, they took them directly to the church and, not being satisfied with the church's response, they have taken them to the general public. . . .
>
> Meanwhile, not having spoken with me for 17 years, they have organized to destroy my reputation and my career.[19]

When the women's allegations were made public, Feltner was dropped as a candidate for a pastoral position in Tennessee and subsequently resigned as lead pastor of a church in Minnesota where he had worked for six years.[20]

TWO OR THREE WITNESSES

Another biblical text that is often misapplied in cases of sexual abuse is 1 Timothy 5:19: "Do not entertain an accusation against an elder unless it is brought by two or three witnesses."[21] Again, as with Matthew 18, an otherwise reasonable biblical standard becomes psychologically and morally inexcusable when applied legalistically to cases of sexual abuse. Think about it: Sexual harassment and abuse do not typically happen in the presence of witnesses.

Consider two well-known cases, for example: Mark Aderholt did not assault Anne Marie Miller in the middle of a youth group meeting; Andy Savage did not have a "sexual incident" with Jules Woodson, a seventeen-year-old girl in his youth group, until he was alone with her in a car on a deserted country road when he was supposed to be driving her home.[22]

Before anyone makes 1 Timothy 5:19 a proof text for a biblical approach to allegations of sexual harassment, abuse, or assault, consider the circumstances with wisdom. Assuming that most men who harass women do it privately, which is more than a fair assumption, one would have to say that this text *almost never* works for sexual allegations against church leaders. In fact, using Matthew 18 and 1 Timothy 5 in such cases is profoundly *un*biblical and profoundly harmful to victims of sexual harassment and abuse.

What is especially tragic, and ironic, in the stories about the Roman Catholic Church, Willow Creek, Sovereign Grace Church, Harvest Bible Chapel, and any number of other examples that could be named, is that *multiple* people came forward—in other words, *more* than two or three witnesses—with enough similarity in their stories, and yet *they still were not believed*. Instead, the wounded were retraumatized by church leaders who responded with biblical law instead of grace, mercy, and discernment.

KEEPING IT IN-HOUSE

A third passage that is sometimes used as an argument for not making allegations public is 1 Corinthians 6:1-8, which reads in part, "If any of you has a dispute with another, do you dare to take it before the ungodly for judgment instead of before the Lord's people? . . . Is it possible that there is nobody among you wise enough to judge a dispute between believers? But instead, one brother takes another to court—and this in front of unbelievers!"[23] This is an important text in which the apostle Paul establishes a godly principle for conflict resolution within the church. But it's also obvious that sexual abuse and sexual harassment are not merely "a dispute between believers." And certainly if the act is criminal, it must be reported to law enforcement and resolved through the legal system. This is a lesson that the church at large has been all too slow to learn.

The answer to how these verses should be applied in situations of abuse involves simple wisdom: The abused don't need to face their abuser—and certainly not one-on-one. And no church should ever demand two or three witnesses for abuse that happens in secret. It's unconscionable and profoundly unbiblical. Moreover, Scripture should never be used to deflect attention away from *what happened* to focus instead on *how* the allegations were brought to light.

Caring for the people involved while pursuing the *truth* with wisdom should always be our objective—even if the truth is ugly. But far too often, churches make decisions that first and foremost protect the institution and its leaders. What will happen to giving, to attendance, to our reputation if this story comes out in public? How a church responds to criticism, or handles information that could damage the reputation of a leader or the church, reveals the culture of that church. Again, compassion, truth, and wisdom should be our guiding lights. But when a culture is toxic, priorities change and truth telling often takes a back seat.

Eventually, however, though it may take a very long time, the truth will come out. When a congregation learns that all the denials, all the spin and alternative narratives were a lie, the church's culture is unmasked as toxic, and the pastor and elders and deacons and other leaders are shown to be complicit—and even intentionally deceptive at times.

The word most often on the lips of Jesus for this was *hypocrisy*. When pastors tell lies, the truth quotient in a church collapses—leading to cynicism, mistrust, and betrayal. When people sit in church on Sunday morning, looking at the pastor and thinking, "What's he hiding?" or "What's the full story?" or "What's really going on with this guy behind closed doors?" the church's credibility collapses. An American scholar of the Vatican put this all into depressingly clear terms:

> The Catholic Church is certainly the organisation that talks most about the truth. The word is always on its lips. It is forever brandishing "truth" around. And at the same time it is an organisation more given to lying than any other in the world.[24]

Pastors, leaders, and congregants in a church with a *tov* culture are free to tell stories that are true. In a toxic church culture, pastors and leaders tell stories that are false, while the congregation either goes along with the deception or lives in blissful ignorance. In the next chapter, we will highlight eight false narratives that churches tell when faced with criticism or allegations of wrongdoing. The spin at work in these narratives is yet another warning sign of a toxic culture taking root.

4

FALSE NARRATIVES

GOD WIRED US AS HUMANS to make sense of our lives through storytelling. We understand our lives—and the lives of our families, our churches, our nation, and our world—by forming the facts (or nonfacts) into a narrative chain. And we live in and through those stories.

Scientists who study the brain and the mind (which are distinct entities for the specialist) tell us that when our brains are not focused on a task, when they are in downtime, our minds naturally go into storytelling mode—weaving an ongoing narrative about the past, present, and future. In a sense, we do not know who we are or how to live until we understand our place in the story.

Lying is a form of storytelling when something goes wrong, a way of "spinning a story" in our own direction, either out of deceit, self-preservation, or self-interest. When something goes wrong in a church—from behind-the-scenes abuses of power to sexual affairs to violence against women to financial sins—the pastor and other leaders often seek to *control* the narrative to protect the reputation of the pastor, the church, or the church's ministries. They may even hire a public relations firm to help them navigate the crisis. But sinful behaviors by church leaders ought not be subject to craftily written words designed to *manage* the narrative. Maybe hiring a PR firm is sometimes necessary for churches. But churches that do can end up sounding like businesses because of carefully crafted statements and avoidance of direct truth-telling. PR folks, after all, are in the business of crafting words. Sadly, however, the desire to manage a crisis and move public opinion often leads to false narratives.

In this chapter, we will dig into eight false narratives that toxic churches often tell to protect themselves and their leaders.[1] Whenever one of these false narratives is used within a church, victims who have brought allegations and wounded resisters who have tried to expose the truth experience *institutional betrayal* and are wounded all over again.[2]

If you fear that a toxic culture is taking root in your church, look for these false narratives when criticisms arise.

1. DISCREDIT THE CRITICS

This false narrative is based on an age-old trick: If you don't want to admit the truth of an accusation, discredit the accuser instead. This can be accomplished by branding the truth tellers as *liars* or seeking to undermine their credibility by attacking their character. We have seen this repeatedly with allegations of sexual abuse in the Roman Catholic Church. Some bishops not only denied the truth, but also attacked the messenger who brought the complaint.

One name for this strategy is *character assassination*. To use a term from the field of logic, this is an *ad hominem* argument—which means to argue based of the *person* rather than the facts. "So-and-so is a bad person; therefore, whatever he or she says is wrong." Or just as commonly, "So-and-so is a *good* person; therefore, whatever he or she says is right." Although a person's character or past behavior can be somewhat predictive, it is essential to determine the *facts and truth* of a situation before making a judgment.

Rachael Denhollander, who blew the whistle on Larry Nassar's sexual abuse and also became an advocate for victims of sexual abuse within Sovereign Grace Ministries, described an all-too-familiar response to abuse:

> When I [came] forward as an abuse victim, this part of my past was wielded like a weapon by some of the elders to further discredit my concern, essentially saying that I was imposing my own perspective or that my judgment was too clouded. . . .
>
> When the Penn State scandal broke, prominent evangelical leaders were very, very quick to call for accountability, to call for change. But when it was within our own community, the immediate response was to *vilify the victims* or to say things that were at times blatantly and demonstratively untrue about the organization and the leader of the organization. There was a complete refusal to engage with the evidence. It did not even matter.[3]

Character assassination seeks to get the congregation to question the truth of the accuser's story by casting doubt on the accuser. Soon, people are pointing fingers at the accuser rather than the abuser. When the accuser becomes the focus of the story, the perpetrators and storytellers score a Pyrrhic victory, and the victim bears the cost.

Another way of discrediting the critics is to question their motives. If you can't get 'em on character, try *collusion*. Everyone loves a good conspiracy theory. We saw this at Willow Creek when Bill Hybels and other church leaders put forth a narrative suggesting that Nancy Beach, Vonda Dyer, Nancy Ortberg, the Mellados, and Betty Schmidt were trying to tarnish Hybels's reputation before he retired. Nancy Beach, on her personal blog, points to "two lengthy family meetings" held at Willow Creek, "complete with timelines and bold statements calling us liars and colluders by name in very specific ways."[4]

Many pastors who have been accused of abusive behavior have persuaded their elder or deacon boards, and even entire churches, to denounce the critics before any credible investigation has even been attempted. Statements such as "She's a loose cannon" or "He's got no Christian maturity" or "She's emotionally unstable" cast a long shadow of doubt over anyone who dares to speak up. When the pastor gains the support of the elders, deacons, or leadership team, the accuser becomes vulnerable. This is one reason why many victims refuse to even come forward.

2. DEMONIZE THE CRITICS

If discrediting the critics through character assassination doesn't work, some churches will take it to the next level by *demonizing* the critics—portraying the accusers as evildoers who are trying to harm the church and all its good work for Christ's Kingdom. Clearly, if the critics are *evil*, they are not to be trusted and one can therefore dismiss what they say about the pastor and the church. Sadly, this strategy often works, as we saw at Harvest Bible Chapel.

Wade Burleson, a courageous pastor who is unafraid to tell the truth about spiritual and sexual abuse in the church, particularly in Southern Baptist circles, devoted a blog post in 2014 to the public "discipline" of three elders who had resigned from the board at Harvest "after speaking out against a 'culture of fear and intimidation' and a lack of transparency in the church, including their concerns over nearly 60 *million dollars* in construction debt."[5] What Burleson quotes here expressly illustrates what it means to demonize one's accusers:

> The elders and Pastor James MacDonald were very
> expressive and deliberate in describing [three former
> elders] to the congregation at Harvest Bible Chapel. They
> used phrases like:
> "What the men are saying is Satanic to the core and
> must be dealt with very directly."
> "We warn the people of Harvest Bible Chapel to
> separate themselves from these false messengers."
> "Please avoid these former Harvest elders at all costs
> lest you incur great detriment to your own soul."[6]

When a church demonizes its critics and appeals to others to avoid these people, its leaders are claiming to be on the side of the angels and God.

3. SPIN THE STORY

Spinning a story is a deceitful strategy designed to hijack the accuser's narrative and create an alternative version—an intentionally false narrative that supports the pastor and the church while creating doubt about the allegations.

Keri Ladouceur is a talented young woman who, beginning in 2007, flourished in youth ministry at Willow Creek, later as a strategic leader across ministries, and ultimately as a leader of community pastors. Keri's accounts of some of her interactions with Bill Hybels over the years differed dramatically from how Hybels and church leadership later portrayed them at Willow Creek's family meetings after the Chicago Tribune story broke. Here is what Keri told me (Laura) about several situations she said were twisted to make Hybels look like an innocent victim or were never told at all.

She attended a leadership conference in California one year with Bill Hybels and several others from the church. One evening, she gathered in the hotel lobby with a group of ten or so friends and colleagues, one of whom said he had a bucket list item to drink a glass of wine with Bill Hybels. Because Keri knew Bill personally from her time at the church, she agreed to send him an email, inviting him to join the group in the lobby. Hybels declined the offer and instead invited Keri up to his room, alone. She immediately declined and rejoined the conversation with her friends in the lobby.

Keri was grateful for Hybels's investment in her, for his contribution to her growth as a leader, a visionary, and a strategic thinker, but certain things about the way he related to her she found distressing. He would often comment on her appearance and her clothes and told her she "lit up the room." Compliments like these from not only a married man, but a pastor and mentor, were confusing to Keri. But she suppressed the mental alarms that went off and decided not to assume salacious intent.

Then, one year during an Easter rehearsal and prayer meeting in the Willow Creek auditorium, Hybels, smelling of alcohol, inappropriately pressed his body against hers and asked her if she thought the vocalist on stage was dressed provocatively. Alarmed, Keri stepped away and later told her husband and a mentor what Hybels had done.

Another time, after a conference in Florida, Keri had a lengthy list of work-related items she wished to discuss with Hybels.

He invited her to discuss the list with him in his car while they drove to the airport. When Keri emailed him to say that a ten-minute car ride would not be enough time to discuss the entire list, Hybels replied that if all Keri wanted to talk about was work, she shouldn't bother coming at all. Something in the exchange seemed amiss to Keri. She talked it over with her husband and responded *no* to Hybels, something Willow Creek employees were trained not to do.

Later, at a 2018 staff meeting in South Haven, Michigan, Hybels again commented on Keri's appearance, noting how her dress accentuated her figure. Keri said this event led her to resign from Willow Creek. Though she loved her job, she was no longer willing to report directly to Bill Hybels.[7]

After her resignation, Keri and her family moved out of state, she took a new job and filed a grievance with Willow Creek's HR department. She also later filed a claim against Willow Creek with the Equal Employment Opportunity Commission for "constructive discharge," an odd term that refers to situations in which an employer "forc[es] an employee to resign by making the work environment so intolerable a reasonable person would not be able to stay."[8]

Now for the spin: Keri told me that when Willow Creek sent one of its elders and an attorney to meet with her to try to convince her to drop her grievance against the church, the attorney acknowledged that Bill Hybels had invited Keri to his hotel room in California, but he insisted that Bill's intentions were simply to be available to Keri for pastoring and mentoring. He told her that if she maintained her "understanding" of the event, he could make it sound as if she had been pursuing Bill. And indeed, that's what happened. At one of Willow Creek's congregational meetings after the *Chicago Tribune* article brought to light the initial allegations against Bill Hybels, Keri said that an elder read incorrectly worded email exchanges between her and Bill and told the congregation that she had pursued Bill at the conference in California. They didn't use Keri's name, but they sought to discredit her nonetheless.[9]

When a woman's story is turned around and people are told that she made up accusations because she wanted someone's job and the church didn't give it to her, that's spin.[10] Or when a pastor tells his congregation that his personal assistant "wanted a bigger challenge than being my assistant" and changed jobs "on good terms," though many insiders know that these words are distortions of the truth, that's spin.[11]

Betty Schmidt, a long-serving elder at Willow Creek, says the church spun a story about her, as well. As she wrote on her personal blog:

> It has been very disturbing to hear my words from the meeting with the WC elders become twisted, added to and extrapolated from. By speaking truth of what I actually said, I hope to make the record clear. The current Willow Creek elders have misquoted and misrepresented me.[12]

It's difficult to believe that the distortions of her story were accidental. It seems more likely they were false narratives designed to protect Bill Hybels and discredit Betty Schmidt.[13]

4. GASLIGHT THE CRITICS

It is hard to imagine a more hurtful strategy than discrediting a person's character, demonizing a truth teller, or spinning a story to create doubt about an accuser; but the practice of gaslighting introduces a vicious psychological element to a false narrative.

The term *gaslighting* comes from the 1938 play *Gas Light*, in which a husband tries to convince his wife she's going crazy—using various techniques, such as dimming the gas lights in their apartment and denying that anything has changed—to cover up his criminal activity. In practice, gaslighting is "a form of psychological manipulation in which a person . . . sows seeds of doubt in a targeted individual, making them question their own memory, perception, or judgment. . . . Using denial, misdirection, contradiction, and misinformation, gaslighting involves attempts to destabilize the victim and delegitimize the victim's beliefs."[14]

Sociologist Paige Sweet emphasizes the *"social* characteristics that actually give gaslighting its power."[15]

> Specifically, gaslighting is effective when it is rooted in social inequalities, especially gender and sexuality, and executed in power-laden intimate relationships. When perpetrators mobilize gender-based stereotypes, structural inequalities, and institutional vulnerabilities against victims with whom they are in an intimate relationship, gaslighting becomes not only effective, but devastating.[16]

When an accuser is gaslighted from the platform of a church, by a trusted pastor with leadership support, the destabilization becomes all the more intense because the prevailing narrative now appears to be connected to God's truth, and it has been broadcast to a crowd of people who accept the church's story. No wonder many accusers choose not to report abuse or back down once they meet resistance.

In an all-too-common example, a woman reports inappropriate behavior toward her by her pastor. Secure in his position of trusted authority, the pastor turns against the woman, saying that she emailed him and invited him to her hotel room, but he resisted her by requesting a phone call instead of a face-to-face meeting. Each of these counteraccusations is designed to get into the woman's head and make her question her own account—what she knows happened—and destabilize her to the point of wondering if she is sane. Some victims back down at this point because of the power differential and how much effort it takes to overcome the pain inflicted by gaslighting.

Writing in *Forbes*, therapist Stephanie Sarkis describes the viciousness of gaslighting even further:

> When gaslighters/narcissists are caught on video saying something that they swore they didn't say, instead of a *mea culpa*, they go on the attack. They will tell you that you heard them incorrectly. Or they'll employ the latest excuse—that the audio was digitally manipulated. A gaslighter/narcissist may also tell you that, yes, he said it, but it was taken "out of context." He may also choose to continue lying without compunction. One thing he will not do is apologize. To a gaslighter/narcissist, an apology is a sign of weakness.[17]

Now for an example. Jules Woodson was seventeen years old when her youth pastor, Andy Savage, took advantage of her. She subsequently mustered the courage to tell Larry Cotton, the church's associate pastor, what Savage had done. In Jules's own words, here is what ensued:

> Just as I had finished telling my story, Larry immediately spoke up and asked me to clarify. He said something to the effect of, "So you're telling me you participated?"
> I remember feeling like my heart had just sunk to the floor. What was he asking? More importantly, what was

he trying to imply? This wave of shame came over me, greater than I had ever felt before. I had just gotten done telling him everything that Andy, my youth pastor, asked me to do. . . . Every ounce of courage I had gathered, to walk in there and tell Larry the truth about what had happened to me, left in an instant. Not only did I suddenly feel this immense guilt for doing what Andy had asked me to do but I also started to feel that this was my fault somehow because I didn't stop him.[18]

In what we view as a classic example of gaslighting, Cotton put Jules on the defensive and destabilized her by turning the situation around, making her feel responsible for what had happened. It would take her almost twenty years to work up the courage to confront her attacker and bring the assault into the public eye.

Survivors of abuse that happens in the church point to contributing factors such as faulty theology, authoritarian leadership, and church leaders who prioritize forgiveness for the abuser above justice and care for the victim. In many cases, pastors are unwilling to consult or refer to licensed therapists because therapists who "operate outside the Bible" might give nonspiritual direction. None of these are excuses for permitting abuse, and they serve only to perpetuate the damaging effects of gaslighting.

5. MAKE THE PERPETRATOR THE VICTIM

Rather than accepting responsibility and apologizing for sin, pastors and church leaders may create false victimization narratives in which everything is reversed and the perpetrators of sexual violence become the victims. Elders, leaders, or other voices of authority at the church may explain how accusers are "not behaving biblically" or are refusing to engage in relationship restoration.

A pastor may lament his weariness or confusion about attacks against his character and against the ministry he spent his life building—and how wounded he was by his accuser going public with the allegations. Or a survivor telling her story to others may be accused of hurtful gossiping or divisiveness. These manipulation narratives are highly effective because they plead sympathy for the evildoer. Suddenly, anger is misdirected and listeners are angry with accusers for their mistreatment of the church or pastor.

We saw this false narrative multiple times in the Willow Creek story. Here is an example from a statement by Bill Hybels at a church family meeting in March 2018:

> My major emotion right now is sadness. I'd always prided myself on being able to build and sustain relationships over a long period of time. . . . The fact that some of these people that you've been reading about—we are not in good relationship right now, and that's very sad to me. I've worked with some of these folks for decades, and they felt like family, like relatives to me. And through the situation that we'll be describing to you, we wound up on different sides of issues, seeing truth in a different way.[19]

The designated spokesperson for the elder board supported Hybels in his victimization narrative:

> We have deep sadness over the broken relationships with people we have respected and people we love. We are grieved for Bill and his family. After 42 years of faithfully pastoring you and me, our congregation, and after his family giving sacrificially, this has been painful beyond words for them.[20]

Hybels, with the support of his elder board, effectively made himself the victim of relational breakdown, as if he were the person harmed instead of the women. "I've spent my whole life trying to *empower women*," he said. "The very fact that a couple women, dating back twenty years, say that my actions or words offended them, is hard for me to hear."[21]

This self-victimization narrative is a textbook example of flipping the script. And it seemed to work. The congregation that night gave Hybels a standing ovation. Many grieved the pain he endured. "I feel so bad for Bill and his family," was a common sentiment. However, Nancy Beach, one of Hybels's victims, saw through this false narrative and responded on her personal blog with her customary clear insight: "Bill Hybels is not the victim here!"[22]

James MacDonald and Harvest Bible Chapel also tried to position themselves as victims when persistent concerns were raised about MacDonald and the leadership of the church. In response to a December 2018 report in *World* magazine that alleged long-standing financial mismanagement, deception, and intimidation at the church, Harvest published a reply on its website that began with the following statement:

It is a sad day when once-credible Christian publications consider the opinions of a few disgruntled former members, already rehashed ad nauseam, of greater weight than the carefully expressed viewpoint of a plurality of local church Elders.

Harvest Bible Chapel has owned its mistakes and endured to become a happier and healthier church, whose members recently pledged—financially, in their walk/work for Christ, and in their promise to share Christ with others—at unprecedented levels. The anticipated attack that comes with God's kingdom moving forward has come, sadly, not from those in the world but from other professing Christians.

We have chosen the high road and refused to engage in public assault on people we once served closely with who just can't seem to "let it go," even after all these years. The Elders are privy to many grace-filled private attempts to reconcile, extended in hopes that these unhappy Christians would find peace.[23]

Wade Mullen, who has researched and written extensively about abuse within the church and how evangelical institutions respond to image-threatening events, analyzed this statement from Harvest Bible Chapel and identified some common tactics that perpetrators use when trying to make themselves out to be the victim. He writes, "Even though the [*World* magazine] story was about specific wrongs done to others, [Harvest] brought attention to their own pain and how 'sad' it was they were being exposed. This tactic . . . is meant to cause others to grant them the compassion and support people would normally give to the wronged."[24]

By referring to the "opinions" of a "few" "disgruntled" "former" members, the church tries to establish the *unfairness* of it all "by suggesting [the accusers] lacked credibility, were motivated by malice, and were alone in their concerns."[25]

Hand in hand with tarnishing the reputation of the accusers, the church seeks to polish its own image—using phrases such as "carefully expressed viewpoint," "a happier and healthier church," "God's kingdom moving forward," "we have chosen the high road," and "grace-filled . . . attempts to reconcile."

Another appeal for sympathy can be seen in the church's reframing of the harm done to others as "mistakes" that the church has now "owned." Wade Mullen notes that "these events are then described as something the leadership had to 'endure,' revealing a perspective that sees one's self as the primary object of harm."[26]

Churches also appeal to their commitment to biblical standards as another means of falsely claiming victim status. Church leadership contends the accusers are behaving contrary to biblical teaching. The church claims the high road because they are following the Bible. The accusers are discredited and the church becomes the victim.

Sovereign Grace Ministries likewise used the Bible to tell abuse victims they should not take believers to court.[27] But ask yourself: Who had something to gain if believers did not go to the legal authorities? Sovereign Grace Ministries and its pastors and leaders. Who had something to lose if the cases weren't taken to the legal authorities? Those abused by the leaders. Those who went public and took their cases to court were seen as victimizing the faithful church people who, out of misapplied biblical convictions, had kept the accusations under wrap.

Leaders may also appeal to protecting the reputation of the church. Again, the church is the victim because accusers are harming its reputation and good work. We saw this type of victimization narrative from the leaders of Sovereign Grace Churches, when they defended themselves against abuse allegations by claiming they were following the Bible:

> The decisions of Rachael [Denhollander] and others to
> publicly pronounce SGC and its pastors guilty of sexual
> abuse and conspiracy, on the basis of false allegations and
> with no direct knowledge of SGC's history or the facts,
> have profoundly damaged the reputations and gospel
> ministries of innocent pastors and churches. . . .

No matter how great the passion for an obviously righteous cause, no fallen human being possesses absolute moral authority, and it benefits neither the victims of sexual abuse nor the name of Christ when believers publicly condemn one another without the facts.[28]

Finally, we especially like Mary DeMuth's tweet about this false victimization narrative:

Let me be clear: To out a predator publicly IS NOT GOSSIP. It's justice. It's protecting more people from being harmed. Brave disclosure is the very essence of God whose heart ALWAYS bends to the vulnerable. To not speak up is sin. Let's flip the narrative, folks.[29]

6. SILENCE THE TRUTH

Sometimes churches create a "silencing narrative" through non-disclosure agreements and membership covenants. This creates the impression, to people who are not in the know, that nothing happened. The church preserves its public reputation, and its false narrative remains intact. Narratives that silence people prevent the truth from becoming known, create confusion for people who sense something is wrong but can't put their finger on it, and sow discord between those who try to speak up and others who choose to believe the false narrative. Silenced truth is an unspoken lie.

Membership covenants, which have become increasingly common in some American churches, are a way for church leaders to prevent negative information from becoming known. The Village Church, a Southern Baptist church in Texas pastored by Matt Chandler, includes a formal dispute resolution clause in its membership covenant.

*Members shall refrain from filing lawsuits against the
Church* and submit to Christian Alternative Dispute
Resolution. In keeping with 1 Corinthians 6:1-8, all
formal disputes, other than those which are subject to the
jurisdiction of the Campus Elders in Article XIII of these
Bylaws, which may arise between any Member of the
Church and the Church itself, or between any Member
of the Church and any Elder, employee, volunteer, agent,
or other Member of this Church, shall be resolved by
mediation, and if not resolved by mediation, then by
binding arbitration under the procedures and supervision
of the Rules of Procedure for Christian Conciliation,
Institute for Christian Conciliation, or similar faith-based
mediation and arbitration group.[30]

This appears to be an attempt to take a biblical approach to conflict resolution, and that's all to the good. Paul told the Corinthians
not to go to public courts to settle their disputes. Surely he thought
the Corinthian legal authorities had some jurisdiction, but he did
not include a list of which matters were for the church to decide
and which were for the courts. The Village Church wants to operate within the parameters of this Pauline directive. What is missing, however, from the bylaws, and what proved to be detrimental
for The Village Church, is a definition of "formal disputes." What
about crimes? Isn't this the very problem so many churches have
had? There is a line, not always fine, between a *dispute* and a *crime*,
and it takes moral sense and discernment to know the difference.
Churches, to put it bluntly, have done poorly here.

Elizabeth Dias of the *New York Times* reported a story about
the Bragg family, who signed the Village Church's membership
covenant, which legally bound them to the covenant and its
bylaws, including Article 10.4. By signing the covenant, the Braggs

promised to "submit to the Bible and to the authority and spiritual discipline of church leaders."[31] But then tragedy struck. In 2017, "Ms. Bragg and her husband, Matt, reported to the Village that their daughter, at about age 11, had been sexually abused at the church's summer camp for children."[32]

There is no evidence that, after learning of the abuse, church leaders disclosed details to the congregation or apologized for this grievous violation of a child. It appeared to the Bragg family that the church preferred to preserve its reputation rather than uncover the truth. A senior director at the church told Ms. Bragg that it was impossible for a staff member to have violated her daughter at camp because the leaders all followed the church's membership covenant. And there was a time when Ms. Bragg would have believed that.

> For years she trusted that her church's top leaders had acted in the best interest of the congregation, and that if she disagreed, the problem was hers. She had a spiritual reason: to doubt them was to doubt God.
>
> But her daughter's ordeal showed her a different side of her church. The Village, like many other evangelical churches, uses a written membership agreement containing legal clauses that protect the institution. The Village's agreement prohibits members from suing the church and instead requires mediation and then binding arbitration, legal processes that often happen in secret. . . .
>
> For months, relatives of the Braggs had been pushing them to hire a lawyer, but the family was nervous. Trusted church friends said hiring a lawyer would not be biblical, citing scripture and the membership covenant.[33]

The Braggs ultimately withdrew their church membership after an arbitration meeting with church representatives led to no resolution, and the family filed a lawsuit against the church in July 2019 after all other options were exhausted.[34] Ms. Bragg said, "What we encountered . . . was a church that has made a conscious choice to protect itself rather than reflect the Jesus it claims to follow."[35] I asked a lawyer friend about these covenants, and this was his response:

> How would this problem have been handled if the victim were an adult who also happened to be a covenant member? The covenant member would bring a lawsuit, and the church would move to compel arbitration in accordance with the membership covenant. The courts would enforce the arbitration agreement because—at least in [name of location]—those types of agreements are sacrosanct. This provides cover of confidentiality so that the dirty laundry is not aired publicly; but more importantly, arbitrators do *not* have to follow the law in reaching their decisions. Arbitration awards can only be overturned in limited circumstances. Advantage: church.[36]

Membership covenants are the not the only tool that churches use to silence people. Another way to prevent negative information from becoming known is through a nondisclosure agreement (NDA). We're not talking about barring someone from taking proprietary information or specialized knowledge from one church to another. No, nondisclosure agreements are designed to silence people who know about bad things that happened behind the scenes and who agree to keep their mouths shut in exchange for some type of severance package or other compensation.

Julie Roys witnessed firsthand the dampening effect of nondisclosure agreements when she was researching her report on Harvest Bible Chapel:

Former Harvest elders, staffers, and members declined to speak on the record, citing nondisclosure and non-disparagement agreements they said Harvest pressured them to sign when they left. In the past several weeks, Harvest also has sent letters to some former employees threatening "legal recourse" should they violate their "agreements with the church."[37]

I (Scot) was in a conversation once with a pastor who told me he'd had to sign an NDA when he left a previous church. When I asked him some questions, all he could say in response was "I won't deny that" or "I would not dispute that." By asking some very direct questions, I was able to glean information even from his indirect answers (which still kept him within the boundaries of his NDA), but the real issue is that people who sign NDAs are often rendered incapable of *establishing justice* by *speaking truthfully* about what they know or have seen or heard. Churches that push NDAs in exchange for a severance package are already in thick with a toxic culture.

Tov churches tell the truth. *Tov* churches do not use NDAs to prevent the truth from being told.

7. SUPPRESS THE TRUTH

A variation of the silencing narrative is suppression of the truth, which may take the form of shaming, intimidation, threatening spiritual or financial consequences, or destruction of evidence.

Sometimes, church leaders will respond to someone who brings an accusation, or even raises a suspicion, by threatening to sue the person, pitting the church's resources against the individual, who may not have the financial wherewithal to withstand a lawsuit. They may also accuse the accuser of sowing discord and division, or "bearing false witness" against one's brother or sister. Or they may announce that they have done an independent investigation that found no wrongdoing, and thus cut off any further inquiry. Asked and answered. They may also appeal to the pastor's or church's reputation to manipulate the victim into silence.

After Wes Feltner got involved with two female students in his youth group, they said they were told to keep quiet to protect their own reputations. When Megan Frey, whose allegations against Feltner included sexual abuse, told the lead pastor what had happened, she said, "There was no empathy. We were all in (the pastor's) office together, telling our story. He cut us off and told us we needed to protect the church because us telling our story would only make us look bad and would only let the church see us for what we really were."[38]

Truth suppression has long been at the heart of the abuse scandals in the Roman Catholic Church. In August 2018, two weeks after the release of the Pennsylvania grand jury report alleging that "church leaders protected more than 300 'predator priests' in six Roman Catholic dioceses across Pennsylvania for decades,"[39] Archbishop Carlo Maria Viganò called for the pope's resignation. One week later, in a homily delivered at the Vatican, Pope Francis "did not specifically address the growing scandal,"[40] but in his remarks he said, "With people lacking goodwill, with people who only seek scandal, who seek only division, who seek only destruction, even within the family: silence, prayer."[41] A Christian's "virtue of silence" seems to be yet another false, truth-suppressing narrative of the Catholic church.

Another way of suppressing the truth is by intimidating the witnesses. Keri Ladouceur said that after she filed a grievance against Bill Hybels with Willow Creek's human resources department, she was told she must sign the report on Willow Creek's campus. Further, she said, she was asked to notify the church when she was close to campus, and again upon arrival. When she pulled into the church parking lot and nervously exited her car, she was confronted almost immediately by Bill Hybels. "Hey, kid," he said. Being intercepted like this felt ominous to Keri. She attempted to dodge Hybels, who tried three times to engage her in conversation. Fortunately, a friend of Keri's was also in the parking lot, and Keri was able to grab the friend's arm and walk into the church with her, crying and shaking.[42]

Senior leaders later signed affidavits denying deliberate intimidation, and Willow Creek claimed that Keri misrepresented the parking lot confrontation (though, again, she was not identified by name). From the main stage at a Willow Creek family meeting, listeners heard this statement: "There was objective evidence, *objective* evidence—email evidence, video footage—to . . . *refute* the allegations."[43] But that video footage was never shared with the congregation.

From our perspective, the most dramatic example of truth suppression also came from Bill Hybels and Willow Creek. A brief elder board review in 2018 uncovered 1,150 emails between Hybels and an unnamed woman. The elders did not evaluate the content of these emails, and the congregation was later told that the emails had been deleted and were unrecoverable. As one of the lead pastors explained it, the emails were not retrievable "just because of the normal deletion time that any corporation or organization" would have. "One thing that the forensic firm was able to find is that these emails weren't physically deleted, these emails naturally went off of the system. . . . No one went in and deleted them."[44]

Bill Hybels also explained the missing email communication at the same congregational meeting:

> As many of you know because you have had very
> confidential interactions with me, the job of a pastor

gets very complicated. . . . I'm in touch with thousands
of pastors . . . and leaders around the world. . . . A lot of
people wanted to contact me about *very* private issues. . . .
I got hacked by a former employee, and all of a sudden I
realized I've got all these emails and a hundred lives could
explode if those emails are made public. . . . I wanted that
level of security so people could confide in me without
worrying about confidentiality.[45]

These explanations about confidentiality and security seemed
perfectly plausible. Subsequently, many people dismissed concerns
about Hybels and the unnamed woman exchanging an excessive
number of emails. It was only after Nancy Ortberg wrote a revealing blog post that the truth began to surface.[46] She described a
meeting between Willow Creek Association board members and
church elders. (For clarity, "both of these women" refers to two
unnamed women who admitted to having inappropriate relationships with Hybels.)

Bill was asked about his "special arrangement with IT,"
where his emails are permanently deleted on a frequent
and regular basis. During that meeting, an Elder told
a WCA Board member that Willow Creek had "no
document retention policy." This was the first time either
Board had heard about this arrangement, but both of
these women told us separately that Bill had told them
about this "special arrangement" years prior.[47]

As a point of reference, most large organizations have policies that dictate how long they will maintain certain documents
(including but not limited to emails and other forms of corre-
spondence) before they are deleted or destroyed. It might be three

years, five years, or seven years, for example, depending on the type of document. Without such a policy at Willow Creek, Bill Hybels and others were free to destroy or delete documents whenever they felt like it.

The real concern here, aside from the lack of controls, is the undisclosed nature of the "special arrangement" Hybels had with the information technology department. We can at least ask if confidentiality was the sole reason for this. Were his emails deleted so that nobody would ever know about the inappropriate content or excessive communication? If it was about confidentiality, as Hybels explained at the family meeting, why wasn't the existence of the arrangement shared openly? Where there is a lack of transparency, there will always be some suspicion.

We saw other examples of information suppression in the Sovereign Grace Churches network. According to a report in *Relevant* magazine, "Former members of SGC say they were discouraged from telling the authorities about instances of sexual abuse at the hands of church leaders and observed leaders scuttling allegations and declining to warn churches about known predators."[48]

When the truth is suppressed and silence is maintained, abusers are able to move on and abuse and wound others. The victim and the silencers are the only ones who know what happened. When silence and suppression become false narratives, the story they tell is that victims don't matter and the abusers' acts are not worthy of discovery.

8. ISSUE A FAKE APOLOGY

Our final false narrative is what we call the *fake apology*, which is really not an apology at all. Fake apologies are not issued out of confession or repentance like a true apology. Instead, they condemn the victim, appease the audience, attach excuses, and try to justify inappropriate behavior. One false narrative begets another. Here, we will briefly summarize the work of Wade Mullen. We recommend further reading from his post "What I've Observed When Institutions Try to Apologize and How They Can Do Better."[49]

The first type of non-apology Mullen identifies is "the apology that condemns" the other person. "The classic example of this is the apology that says, 'I'm sorry you feel that way.'"[50] There is no admission of wrongdoing, only a manipulative suggestion that the other person is either too sensitive or has misinterpreted the situation.

The next "apology" is one that appeases. "It is not an attempt to do all that is necessary to right wrongs, but an attempt to offer only what is needed to quell [an] outcry."[51]

Third is the "apology" that comes with excuses attached. Mullen calls this an "apoloscuse." It can take many forms, but they all seek to shift the blame or one's perception of the evildoer. Churches may say it was "never our intention" to slander a truth teller, or "it was outside of our control." The excuse eviscerates the apology, rendering it meaningless.

Churches may seek to justify the behavior, thereby rendering another non-apology. They may try to suggest that a leader's sins are "not that bad," or that the woman should have known not to be alone with a male pastor, or that her husband should have intervened.

Mullen also identifies "apologies" that are couched in terms of self-promotion. "Many public statements of apology . . . become pitches for why [the organization is] still worthy of continued support and engagement from [its] followers."[52] Mullen adds that organizations should never announce that they are "on the same side as the victims." That decision, he says, is only for the victims to make.

Finally, Mullen describes non-apologies that attempt to garner sympathy for the institution. This is the "we're hurting too" type of statement that tends to "displace the pain of the wounded with the pain of the wounder."[53]

Bottom line, a cheap apology is not an apology at all. It is a false narrative that only claims to be doing the right thing while in fact it tries to excuse, appease, or justify sin and garner sympathy for the sinner. Authentic apologies include surrender, confession, ownership, recognition, and empathy. "And out of that broken place," says Mullen, "might emerge the words, 'We are so sorry.'"[54]

✳ ✳ ✳

Okay, enough of that. We believe we have offered enough examples and evidence of a toxic culture that prevails in far too many churches. Let us now turn our attention to finding a way forward. In what follows, we will provide a map to a culture of goodness (*tov*), so that we can learn to measure our churches the way God does—by how *tov* they are.

PART 2

THE CIRCLE
OF *TOV*

How great is the goodness
you have stored up for those who fear you.
You lavish it on those who come to you for protection,
blessing them before the watching world.

PSALM 31:19

The truth is like a lion. You don't have to defend it.
Let it loose and it will defend itself.

ST. AUGUSTINE

No matter how complex and extensive the cultural system
you may consider, the only way it will be changed is by an
absolutely small group of people who innovate
and create a new cultural good.

ANDY CROUCH, *CULTURE MAKING*

You are a chosen people. You are royal priests, a holy nation,
God's very own possession. As a result, you can show others
the goodness of God, for he called you out of the darkness
into his wonderful light.

1 PETER 2:9

CREATING A GOODNESS CULTURE

CHURCH CULTURE MATTERS. As we live *in* our culture and also *into* our culture, our culture begins to live in and into us. A good culture will shape us toward goodness; a toxic culture will shape us toward evil. Yes, we can resist and change the culture of a church, but resisting, at times, is like trying to slow down a hurricane.

How we understand and *feel* about our relationship with God is formed and fostered by the culture of the church we're in. We tend to equate how we stand with the leaders of the church, and how we stand with the congregation—that is, our conformity to what they approve and disapprove—with how we stand with God. Sometimes the standard is overtly taught from the pulpit: "This is the type of people we want to be." More often, approval or disapproval is communicated in subtler ways, such as through the passages of Scripture that are taught or not taught, who gets to be on the platform on Sundays, who is selected for leadership, or the prevailing narrative about how the church should interact with the world.

We may like to *think* of ourselves as rugged individualists, but we aren't. We are who we are in relationship with others. If a church is corrupted or toxic in its relationships, it will have corrupted and toxic categories of approval. If a church is good and healthy in its relationships, it will have good and healthy categories of approval. No church is perfect, of course—there will always be a combination of corruption and goodness—but we must continually strive for goodness because the environment will transform us into who we become. The longer we stay in a church, the more we will absorb the church's culture. This is why David Brooks warns us in *The Second Mountain* never to underestimate the power of a culture to shape us.

Let's be clear about one thing from the outset: Choosing a church is choosing a culture, and the culture we choose will form us into the people we become. So rather than choosing a church based on who preaches on Sunday morning, or who leads worship, or what type of music we prefer, we would be wise to make our selection based on the *culture* of the church community. In this chapter, we will sketch the major elements of a *good* church culture, what we're calling *a culture of tov.*

JESUS UNDERSTANDS CULTURE

Let's start by reading a mini-sermon by Jesus about how culture shapes people. He uses a little analogy about how what enters through the eye transforms the entire body.

> Your eye is like a lamp that provides light for your body. When your eye is healthy, your whole body is filled with light. But when it is unhealthy, your body is filled with

darkness. Make sure that the light you think you have is not actually darkness. If you are filled with light, with no dark corners, then your whole life will be radiant, as though a floodlight were filling you with light.[1]

Permit us to suggest a flexible reuse of these words of Jesus. The eye of our church's culture provides light for the whole church. If our church's eye is healthy, the whole church culture will be filled with light. If our church's eye is unhealthy, the whole church culture will be filled with darkness. When our church is filled with light, the life of the church life be radiant. Culture matters because the light of that culture pervades.

A SURPRISING RESPONSE TO A BLOG POST

On my (Scot's) *Jesus Creed* blog on July 9, 2018, I briefly presented the need for churches to intentionally nurture a goodness culture.[2] I was surprised by the number of people who wrote or spoke privately to me about the meaningfulness of the words *good* and *goodness*. Why was it meaningful to propose that churches must be *good*? Why was it surprising to so many that we should strive for *goodness*?

Here's why: We aren't comfortable with the word *good* when it comes to our self-claims. For many, to say, "I am good" is the height of arrogance. One of the implications of Protestant theology is that any talk of being good is inappropriate, a devious theological error, or at least unchristian boasting. A Bible verse I learned back in the King James Version days of my childhood—"there is none that doeth good, no, not one"[3]—is central to a passage in Romans 3 where Paul quotes the Old Testament to show how the law establishes our sinfulness. In this context, Paul strings together a series of virtues that we, as sinners, ought not claim for ourselves:

No one is righteous.
No one is truly wise.
No one seeks God.
No one does good.
No one knows the way of peace.
No one fears God.[4]

Because everyone is caught in a massive network of sin, no one can stand before God and say, "I am good." It's against the Bible.

Or is it?

This bold denial of our goodness is not the whole story. Even though we are not good, God flips everything upside down and calls us to *do* good and *be* good and to be known for *good works*. How do we reconcile "no one is good" with "so be good"? We are not good in and of ourselves. We cannot manufacture our own goodness. Doing good and being good are possible *only* by God's empowering grace.[5] Goodness is one of the manifestations of the Holy Spirit's presence in our lives.[6]

Because goodness is so vital to this book, we want to take time to develop an understanding of what the Bible says about it.[7]

THE BIG IDEAS ABOUT *TOV*

Tov, the Hebrew word for "good" or "goodness," is by far one of the most popular terms in the Bible. With more than 700 occurrences of the word in Scripture, we could say that our Bible is the Book of *Tov*. Surely these poetic lines from the prophet Amos reveal the importance of goodness for those who hear God's call:

Do what is *tov* and run from evil
so that you may live!
Then the LORD God of Heaven's Armies will be your helper,

just as you have claimed.
Hate evil and love what is *tov*;
turn your courts into true halls of justice.[8]

From the very first page of our Bibles, *tov* is the Bible's summary term, the "executive virtue," for how God wants us to live. *Tov* stretches out in several directions, so let's break it down into its separate themes.

God alone is tov

Goodness, or *tov*, is first and foremost about God: God **is** *tov*. The psalmist declares it: "You are *tov* and do only *tov*."[9] When God chose to reveal his glory to Moses, he hid him in a crack in a crag on Mount Sinai and said, "I will make all my *tov* pass before you, and I will call out my name, Yahweh, before you."[10] When God's *tov* passed by Moses, the palm of God's hand protected Moses from being undone by the sheer intensity of God's glory. As God's *tov* passed by, he announced his name: YHWH. Thus, God's *tov* became inextricably connected to his name. That's how vital *tov* is in the Bible.

God **is** *tov* and God **does** *tov*—often referring to God's covenant making and generous acts of salvation. "Not a single one of the *tov* promises the LORD had given to the family of Israel was left unfulfilled; everything he had spoken came true."[11] Not only is God good, but he pursues us with his goodness: "Surely your *tov* and unfailing love will pursue me all the days of my life"[12] Don't miss this: God relentlessly and tenaciously *chases* us with *tov*. Those who turn to him for refuge are invited to "taste and see that the LORD is *tov*."[13] Those who taste this *tov* can also say, "How *tov* it is to be near God!"[14]

Those who turn and taste and draw near soon discover that the

God of *tov* is full of divine love. So let us join our voices and sing along with King David: "O Lord, you are so *tov*, so ready to forgive, so full of unfailing love for all who ask for your help."[15] *Tov* is a major word in the Bible because the God of the Bible is completely *tov*.

God's design is tov

Tov is God's design for all creation. He shapes everything for goodness. His turning of the "formless and empty"[16] into created order gave everything he created a design, a purpose, a function. *Tov* is God's artistic evaluation of all he did.[17] In other words, perfect, excellent, just as I wanted! Put differently, *tov* is about beauty, aesthetics, excellence, and what pleases our senses of sight and sound. Like a well-played piano, a coordinated golf swing, the right word for the right situation, a European cathedral that stands above all structures and beckons us to come pray and worship, a beautifully arranged dining room, a well-organized event, a jolly beagle following its nose across the lawn. All *tov*. *Tov* suggests what is visually pleasing and pleasant, what is desirable, what is of high quality, and what is excellent. When everything is in its place doing its proper task, we say, *Tov*!

When we live according to God's design, we become people who *love*. God's ultimate design is for us is love. When an expert in the law asked Jesus what it takes to receive God's approval, what did Jesus tell him? Love God and love others.[18] This is what I (Scot) have called "the Jesus Creed."[19] Loving God and loving others is "all" we are called to do—though it is an *all* that goes to the depths of our being and transforms our character into love. To love is *tov*.

God's design for us comes to fruition through a *Spirit-soaked*, *Spirit-filled*, and *Spirit-directed* life. Love is the first fruit of the Spirit, and all who are open to the Spirit will love God and love others. All who are open to the Spirit will be filled with *tov*.

A *tov* life develops in us over time. No one, at least no one we've ever met, wakes up on day one of the Christian life instantly, permanently, deeply loving. Over time, in accordance with God's design for us, and by the inner working of God's Spirit in our lives, we develop a *tov* character—a character that God can approve. A *tov* character is formed by Spirit-filled *tov* behavior, and those who have a *tov* character will behave in *tov* ways. In other words, *tov* is *active*.

Tov *is active*

Tov is God's design for our moral virtues. *Tov* is something that happens, something visible. When the apostle Peter summarized the public ministry of Jesus, he said, "You know that God anointed Jesus of Nazareth with the Holy Spirit and with power. Then Jesus went around *doing good* and healing all who were oppressed by the devil, for God was with him."[20] The Greek word behind the phrase "doing good" is *euergetes*, which comprises *eu* (meaning "good" or *tov*) and *ergetes* (working, doing deeds). In John 10:11, Jesus refers to himself as the "the good shepherd." Jesus lived a life of observable goodness because he was inherently good. The *tov* Messiah naturally went around doing *tov*.

We can say this even more emphatically: Jesus doesn't just **do** *tov*; he **is** *tov*. When we look at Jesus, we see *tov*. To be like Jesus (Christlike) is to be *tov*; and to be *tov* is to be like Jesus.

The theme of actively doing *tov* runs throughout the Bible. Solomon's famous petition to God includes a pristine summary of how to live in the presence of our *tov* God: He prays that God will "teach [your people Israel] the *tov* way in which they should walk."[21] God's people are to walk in "the *tov* way," the way of God's beautiful design for us. Jesus taught us to "do good" to our enemies and to be people who produce "good fruit."[22]

But remember, we don't make ourselves into *tov* people. God transforms us through the power of his Holy Spirit, for whom *goodness* is a natural fruit.[23] The apostle Paul tells the Roman Christians, in a moment of clear encouragement, "I am fully convinced, my dear brothers and sisters, that you are full of goodness."[24] Writing to the Ephesians, Paul echoes his word to the Galatians about the fruit of the Spirit when he says, "The fruit of the light consists in all *goodness*, righteousness and truth."[25] Over and over, the New Testament calls us to be people shaped into *goodness*, and this term is the New Testament equivalent of the Old Testament *tov*.[26] Say it aloud: "The fruit of the Spirit is *tov*."

The foremost expression of *tov* is *generosity*. In the parable of workers in the vineyard, in Matthew 20:1-15, the owner (who represents God in the story) says, "Are you envious because I am *generous*?"[27] In the ESV, it reads, "Do you begrudge my *generosity*?"[28] The Greek word behind these italicized terms is *agathos*, another word for *good*. If it were in Hebrew, it would be *tov*. To be *tov* is to be generous. Generosity's next-door neighbors are integrity, faithfulness, graciousness, and kindness.

To be *tov* is to be a person who, from the inside out, consistently does what is right and generous. A *tov* culture forms when individuals are *tov* and do acts of *tov*.

Not long ago, I (Scot) read a story about one of my favorite NCAA men's basketball coaches, Tony Bennett of the University of Virginia. After his team won its first-ever national championship in 2019, Bennett was offered a contract extension and a raise by the university. He accepted the additional year, but he had a different idea about the money. When you read his story below, you may have the same response I had: That's *tov*!

Tony Bennett declined to take a raise while extending his contract by another year.

The Cavaliers announced the extension Monday, saying Bennett asked for the money to be used to pay his staff more and for improvements to both his program as well as other Virginia athletic teams.

"[My wife] Laurel and I are in a great spot, and in the past I've had increases in my contract," Bennett said in the news release. "We just feel a great peace about where we're at, all that's taken place, and how we feel about this athletic department and this community and this school. I love being at UVA. . . .

"I have more than enough, and if there are ways that this can help out the athletic department, the other programs and coaches, by not tying up so much [in men's basketball], that's my desire." . . .

"Tony's decision—to turn down a well-deserved raise and instead invest in his players and UVA athletics more broadly—tells you everything you need to know about him as a leader and as a human being," university president Jim Ryan said. "Tony is one of the most selfless people I've ever met, and this is just the latest example."[29]

Tov is generosity, and generosity is *tov*. Tony Bennett demonstrated what it means to actively pursue *tov*. This kind of behavior helps to form a culture of *tov* on a team, in the athletic department, and in a school. Individuals acting out goodness help to form a goodness culture.

Tov *resists evil*

The apostle Paul encourages us to practice the divine design of *tov*. He says we are designed by God to do *tov*: "For we are God's masterpiece. He has created us anew in Christ Jesus, so we can *do the good things* he planned for us long ago."[30] Peter, likewise, exhorts the church to practice *tov*—to "silence the ignorant talk of foolish people," even in the face of fear and suffering.[31] "Those who suffer according to God's will should commit themselves to their faithful Creator and continue to do good."[32] Peter also says that we are to "submit [ourselves] for the Lord's sake to every human authority" whose purpose is "to commend those who do right."[33]

As we mentioned above, we Protestants are nervous about applying the word *good* to human beings. Some translations of 1 Peter reflect this uneasiness, substituting words such as *honorable* or *right* instead of *good*. But each of these verses in 1 Peter uses the word for *good* or *doing good*.

The fruit of the Spirit begins with love and includes goodness, but if we focus only on the positive traits mentioned in Galatians 5:22-23 and overlook the "acts of the flesh" described in verses 19-21, we might miss an important point: Each aspect of the fruit of the Spirit is also *an act of resistance*. To do *tov* requires us to resist what is not *tov*, what is bad and evil and corrupt. To live in the Spirit is to resist the works or acts of the flesh. Over and over, the Bible teaches us to pursue goodness and turn away from evil. "The acts of the flesh are obvious," writes Paul, and he lists such things as sexual immorality, hatred, jealousy, fits of rage, and selfish ambition.[34] To live a life of *tov* means resisting the sinfulness and toxicity of these acts of the flesh.

Resisting evil resonates deeply in the Bible: Right from the outset, good (*tov*) is set in opposition to evil (*ra*): "In the middle of the garden [God] placed . . . the tree of the knowledge of *tov* and *ra*."[35] God alone knows the depth of *tov* and *ra*.[36] If *tov* points us toward God's desire for his designed creation, *ra* points us in the opposite direction.

Like God, the future Messiah would know the difference between *tov* and *ra*;[37] so too those whom the prophet knows are blessed.[38] The disobedient will keep "following the stubborn desires of their evil [ra] hearts,"[39] so the psalmist tells us to "turn from ra and do tov."[40] Proverbs 14:22 makes this promise: "If you plan to do ra, you will be lost; if you plan to do tov, you will receive unfailing love and faithfulness." Those who do what is tov will turn their backs on what is ra. To do one is to resist the other.

GOD'S ULTIMATE APPROVAL

Tov is a one-word summary of God's ultimate approval. He doesn't give letter grades. Nowhere in the Bible does it say that Moses got an A, David got a B, Solomon a C, Isaiah an A, Paul an A, and Peter . . . well, he pulled it together at the end and got an A-minus. No, God's final approval rating is simply tov.

When God spoke from heaven at the baptism of Jesus and said, "This is my Son, whom I love; with him I am well pleased," that was tov.[41] The life of Jesus? Tov. The teachings of Jesus? Tov. The accomplishment of his death, resurrection, and ascension? Tov. In Christ, it's all tov.

When the church lives as God designs, we hear God's wonderful "Tov!" When we parent as God designs, when we work as God wants us to work, when we love as God shaped us to love . . . tov! When we live, act, and speak as God designs, we can listen for his ultimate approval: Tov!

God's tov can be heard in the parables of Jesus when he says, "Well done!"[42] To top it off, Jesus refers to the servants in the parable as "good and faithful." That's tov again. Luke describes a man named Joseph as "good and righteous,"[43] and this serves as a comprehensive evaluation of his character. Tov!

Tov encompasses the span of history. At Creation, God looked at his handiwork, and when he got everything right where he wanted it, he gave it his ultimate stamp of approval: "Tov!"

Fast-forward to the final judgment, and there is only one word we want to hear: *Tov!* *Tov* is all that matters. *Tov* is divine design and divine evaluation. It is divine pleasure, divine attractiveness, and divine satisfaction.

THE *TOV* GOSPEL

One more observation—kind of a sidebar, but it's something to think about: The word *gospel* could be translated as "the message of *tov.*" The word is often rendered as "Good News," and that's accurate. The Greek word combines "good" (*eu*) with "declaration" (*angelos*), and that little Greek *eu* is the same word sometimes used to translate the Hebrew word *tov.*[44] Add this up and here's what we've got: The gospel is the message of *tov.* The gospel is about God's *tov* coming to us in Jesus, who is *tov*, and thus making *us* into agents of *tov.*

If we understand the impact that our church's culture has on us, we must not underestimate the importance of creating a *tov* culture. God designed all creation and everything in it—including you and me and our churches—for *tov.* *Tov* is both the design and the ultimate approval rating from God.

JESUS, THE ONE TRUE MAN OF *TOV*

What every church needs is a model of goodness—in its pastors, its leaders, its people. It will come as no surprise that the perfect example of *tov* is Jesus. Pick up your Bible and read Matthew 8–9 and you will see *tov* in action. Jesus is approachable, willing, compassionate, and humble.[45] He teaches, encourages, admonishes, and challenges. He heals, forgives, and restores because he sees and he listens. He also models *tov* as *resistance* to *ra*—touching the "unclean," dining with tax collectors "and other disreputable sinners," confronting evil in people's hearts, casting out evil spirits "with a simple command," and healing "all the sick."[46] And then this summary statement: "Jesus traveled through all the towns and villages . . . announcing the Good News about the Kingdom."[47] He did all this because God was *with* him, and *in* him, and working *through* him to accomplish the *tov* gospel for all of us.

Jesus knew God's *design* on his life: to live and to die and to be raised for others. His entire life was lived for others. Jesus was a good and beautiful man of *virtues* shaped by God's design, and nothing illustrates his virtues more than the Beatitudes, the section of his Sermon on the Mount where he blesses all the "wrong" people (in the eyes of the world) and assigns to them a special place with God. The people he blesses are marked by a way of life:

> God blesses those who are poor and realize their need
>> for him,
>>> for the Kingdom of Heaven is theirs.
> God blesses those who mourn,
>> for they will be comforted.
> God blesses those who are humble,
>> for they will inherit the whole earth.
> God blesses those who hunger and thirst for justice,
>> for they will be satisfied.
> God blesses those who are merciful,
>> for they will be shown mercy.
> God blesses those whose hearts are pure,
>> for they will see God.
> God blesses those who work for peace,
>> for they will be called the children of God.
> God blesses those who are persecuted for doing right,
>> for the Kingdom of Heaven is theirs.
>
> God blesses you when people mock you and persecute
> you and lie about you and say all sorts of evil things

against you because you are my followers. Be happy about it! Be very glad! For a great reward awaits you in heaven. And remember, the ancient prophets were persecuted in the same way.[48]

Jesus' life on earth ended in a gruesome death. But that death was utterly reversed by a resurrected life so strong that it shattered the grip of sin and death. Jesus ascended with his Father's *approval*—that's *tov!*—to rule at the right hand of God Almighty. A life designed for death, a death designed for life, and the virtues of utter goodness in what he taught and how he lived. That's Jesus, the one truly *tov* and beautiful one.

CREATING A *TOV* CHURCH

If we as individuals in the church will pursue Jesus' *tov* way of life, we will help to create a *tov* church culture. A "church called *tov*" is designed by God to accomplish his purpose in the world by doing it his way. We don't create *tov* churches in our own strength, by grit and determination or by clever programming. *Tov* churches are the work of God's Spirit set free to create *tov*—and the eight other fruitful attributes outlined by Paul in Galatians 5. What God has in mind is a loving, joyful, peaceful, patient, kind, *tov*, faithful, and self-controlled body of believers about whom he can say, "That's it! That's what I designed! That's excellent! That's good! That's *tov!*"

In the chapters ahead, we will look at seven key elements of a *tov* culture: (1) empathy and compassion, (2) grace and graciousness, (3) putting *people* first, (4) truth telling, (5) justice, (6) service, and (7) Christlikeness. A toxic culture will resist a *tov* culture, but a *tov* culture, by the power of the Holy Spirit, will go to battle and overcome a toxic culture.

THE CIRCLE OF *TOV*
Nurturing Habits of Goodness

Nurture Christlikeness
Resist the leader culture

Nurture empathy
Resist a narcissist's culture

Nurture service
Resist the celebrity culture

TOV

Nurture grace
Resist a fear culture

Nurture justice
Resist the loyalty culture

Put people first
Resist institution creep

Tell the truth
Resist false narratives
Know Yom Kippur
Form a truth-telling culture

6

TOV CHURCHES NURTURE EMPATHY

JESUS HAD AN EYE ON THE WOUNDED. When he preached his first sermon in his hometown synagogue, he read from the prophet Isaiah:

> The Spirit of the Lord is upon me,
>   because he has anointed me
>   to bring good news to the *poor*.
> He has sent me to proclaim release to the *captives*
>   and recovery of sight to the *blind*,
>   to let the *oppressed* go free,
> to proclaim the year of the Lord's favor.[1]

We don't know all the details—why Jesus was the reader that day or why this text was the one he read—but we know this:

The text and Jesus were a match made in heaven. This was a *tov* moment. The prophet Isaiah's stunning prediction of what God would do to restore the fortunes of his people aligned perfectly with the mission and heart of Jesus for his people in Galilee. He came to "bring good news [the message of *tov*] to the poor" and "proclaim release [forgiveness, liberation] to the captives." He would give "sight to the blind" and freedom to "the "oppressed." The heart of Jesus' mission is the wounded, the neglected, the ignored, the abused, the lost, the violated. He sees them because he has the eyes of God.

By all accounts, one word that describes Jesus to the core is *empathy*, which is one part of the word translated "compassion" in our English Bibles. Empathy is the ability to feel what someone else feels, to exit our own feelings and enter the experience of others. Thus, empathy is the ability to see the world through others' pain. Faithful to the calling on his life given by the God of empathy, Jesus was faithfully compassionate to everyone he met.

COMPASSION IS THE OUTWORKING OF EMPATHY

During the writing of this book, yet another horrific story of gun violence hit the news when a lone gunman shot and killed twenty-two people at a Walmart in El Paso, Texas. Among the victims was Margie Reckard, a sixty-three-year-old woman who was shopping for groceries as she did every Saturday.

Margie and her husband, Antonio Basco, had no relatives and few friends in the El Paso area. Margie's children from a previous marriage lived elsewhere. Alone and heartbroken, Basco brought flowers each day to a makeshift memorial outside the store, and he spent long hours there, often from morning until dark. Sometimes he returned at night and slept on the ground next to the memorial. Photographs showed Basco's obvious distress as he slumped weeping at the loss of his wife, total anguish on his face.

Basco told Salvador Perches, the funeral director, about his fears. His fear that he was now alone. His fear about not having a family because Margie was all he had. His fear that nobody would attend his wife's funeral. When Perches shared a message on Facebook, along with a photo of Basco at Margie's memorial site, it soon went viral. The message read: "Mr. Antonio Basco was married for twenty-two years to his wife Margie Reckard. He had no other family. He welcomes anyone to attend his wife's services. . . . Let's show him and his wife some El Paso love."[2]

Empathy went viral, and compassion followed it. *Tov* blanketed El Paso.

On the day of the visitation, more than three thousand people showed up, some waiting hours to envelop Antonio Basco in hugs, share heartfelt condolences, and bring him gifts. At Margie's funeral, the last of the twenty-two victims' funerals, Basco entered a venue packed with four hundred supporters. Seven hundred more people waited outside in the Texas heat to express their condolences to the grieving husband, the line wrapping around the block for half a mile. Neighbors set up food and water stations for those waiting in line.

One supporter flew in from San Francisco to attend the funeral of a woman she had never met, and to support a widower she had never seen. Another woman drove six hours and then waited an additional two hours to tell Basco, whom she had never met, that she loved him and that he wasn't alone.[3] El Paso resident Victor Perales said that he and his wife came to the funeral "to give [Basco] a hug and let him know we can be his family."[4] There were hundreds just like them. More than nine hundred flower arrangements and ten thousand condolence messages arrived from as far away as New Zealand, Norway, and Japan. And a GoFundMe campaign organized by journalist Carlos Armendariz, who took photos of Basco at the memorial site that went viral, raised more than $41,000 from 1,425 donors.[5]

Basco said he had never felt so much love in his entire life. "So many people put their arms around me, grieved with me, cried with me, it touched my heart," he said at the cemetery. "I love you and I'm proud and I'm honored to have you all here as my family."[6]

The mark of empathy is to feel another's pain; the mark of compassion is "having the desire to alleviate or reduce the suffering of another" and to do something about it.[7] The community of El Paso saw Antonio Basco's pain. They saw his suffering. They saw him standing alone and moved to comfort him and be with him. That's *tov*!

The church is designed by God to be a *tov* culture filled with empathy and compassion. The church is designed by God to wrap its arms around the poor, the oppressed, and the needy of this world because, like Jesus, we want to alleviate their pain.

THE CIRCLE OF *TOV*
Nurturing Habits of Goodness

Nurture empathy
Resist a narcissist's culture

TOV

NURTURING A CULTURE OF EMPATHY

Any church that claims connection to Jesus, and any church that wants to follow Jesus, absolutely must have a heart for the wounded and the marginalized. Sadly, many churches lack empathy and therefore lack compassion.

Here are some examples of people who may experience a lack of empathy and compassion. As we commit ourselves to pursuing a *tov* culture in our churches, these can become *opportunities* for us to resist such actions by forming a culture rooted in empathy and compassion.

- Women who are not permitted to use their gifts in the church.
- Women—and others—who are not believed when they share about abuse at the hands of church leaders.
- Widows who seem to slide from hearty participation to the back pew (or even out the door) when their husbands pass away.
- Widowers who, though not as numerous as widows, find themselves lonely in the church.
- The physically challenged, who sometimes can't even get into the church building because the facility doesn't meet code.
- The depressed, the anxious, and the obsessive-compulsive, who are reluctant to share their private struggles.
- The elderly, who often are ignored or met with impatience.
- The divorced, who feel they don't belong or are being judged.
- Those from different economic levels who sometimes cannot participate in "churchwide" events because of a lack of resources.

- Those who differ ethnically or racially from the mainstream, dominant, or privileged culture in the church.
- Others who stand out from the prevailing demographics of the church.

Churches that follow Jesus don't simply take up a cause for one specific group; they develop a culture in which they hear the cries of all the distressed, all the wounded, and respond with compassion. Circle of *Tov* churches will develop an "empathy radar" with an instinctive bias toward acts of grace, peace, mercy, and goodness for everyone.

A goodness culture, if it's truly good, will touch all corners of the church. Though here we will focus primarily on how churches can become more empathetic toward women—because of what has happened to women in so many churches—everything we say can equally be applied to racism, classism, and other isms that degrade our fellow divine-image bearers. How the church treats women is often a barometer of its culture and how it will treat people in general. And when you consider that women make up more than half the congregation in most churches, it seems like a natural place to start when seeking to develop a culture of *tov* in the church.

The Circle of *Tov* begins with empathy and compassion. The absence of these qualities increases the chances that the church's culture will be abusive toward women and others in the congregation. If churches will become deeply empathetic toward women and other groups that are often marginalized, if pastors will become more empathetic, we believe that a completely different culture—one marked by *tov*—will begin to take root. In such a culture, women's giftings will flourish, their voices will be heard, and they will be safe. In such a culture, women will become far more visible—and valued.

Women who seek to exercise their gifts in the church are

sometimes perceived as a threat by narcissistic pastors who are wrapped up in the power game and surrounded by sycophantic supporters who are determined to protect their male-centric culture.[8] Does that sound too strong? Witness the "Go home!" posture taken by John MacArthur, a prominent and powerful male leader.[9] Such attitudes have driven women out of the church and into the marketplace, where their gifts are able to flourish. Women who are silenced in the church can and do become significant voices outside the circle of a male-centric church culture. But how much better it would be if they weren't silenced in the first place.

Often, the culture in the church merely reflects the culture in society at large. And so often it's been true that a male-centric Western culture undervalues or overlooks the contributions of women.

Not far from 10 Downing Street in London is a monument to the Women of World War II. Belatedly constructed in 2005—*sixty* years after the war ended—the twenty-two-foot-high bronze monument sits in the middle of Whitehall, one of London's busier streets.[10] Arrayed along the upper half of the monument and stretching around all four sides are castings of seventeen uniforms or types of clothing worn by women in helping the British fight the Axis powers of Europe. They look as if they've been hung on pegs, and indeed the artist's vision was to suggest the idea of "these women hanging up their uniforms and going back to their normal lives after the end of the war."[11]

What struck me forcefully, as I (Scot) stood on the sidewalk observing the sculpture, was that there were no faces and no names on the monument. All those women—nearly seven million by some counts—who had contributed so much to the war effort, have been reduced to the clothing they wore and the duties they performed. These nameless, faceless women of World War II symbolize society's silencing as well.

Because most churches have a male-centric culture—whether it's because of narcissistic male leadership or simply due to a particular reading of the New Testament—women are often invisible contributors: useful but not central, necessary but not necessarily valued. Yes, there is a long history of biblical discussion and theological debate about the "proper role" of women in the church—what they can and can't do—but that is well beyond the scope of this present work. What we're addressing here is *how people are treated* in the church, and we are advocating for a culture of empathy and compassion. Women don't always experience much of either.

A church called *tov* will empower women (and others) in their giftedness and encourage those gifts to flourish within the body of Christ and in the world. In a culture of empathy and compassion, people will not be made to feel invisible. They will be *seen* and *heard*. When they bring their woundedness with them, they will be embraced and enfolded and responded to with grace and mercy. And if they bring allegations of abuse, they will be believed and comforted and supported—and the truth will be pursued and upheld, even (or maybe especially) if it leads to the courts of power. The *tov* church will not protect the institution at the expense of the individual. The *tov* church will not spin false narratives to hide what has happened and protect the abusers. And the *tov* church will do everything it can not to re-wound the wounded. Empathy and compassion demand no less.

NURTURING WOMEN IN THE CHURCH

How can we form a culture of *tov* in which women (and others) are honored and valued and given a voice? What can we do to reshape a male-centric culture into a more balanced male-and-female-based culture that reflects a Christlike culture of *tov*?[12]

What we want is to be a church in which *every person* is equally valued as an image-bearer with gifts and abilities empowered by the Holy Spirit. How can we work toward such a culture?

Let's remember how cultures are formed: Leaders form and tell a preliminary narrative, act out or model values for others to see and emulate, teach the important principles of faith and practice, and articulate policies that reinforce the values of the organization. These narratives, actions, principles, and policies are then retold, reenacted, retaught, and re-formed by the congregation.

Because it all begins with a narrative, with the stories we tell, the way to begin forming a new culture of empathy and compassion is by learning to tell a new story.

First, a church that is committed to developing a culture of *tov* will *know the names and stories of women in the Bible.* We've probably all heard sermons about Esther or Ruth, who both have Bible books named after them. But what about some of the lesser-known women who played significant roles? What does the average churchgoer know about Leah or Rebekah, Miriam or Abigail, Deborah or Huldah, Lydia or Priscilla, Phoebe, Junia, or the daughters of Philip?

Sure, the information in the Bible about some of these women is scant compared to some of the men. But let's be honest. If a best-selling book can be written about Jabez, whose story commands roughly seventy words of Scripture (depending on the translation), certainly we can find some valuable lessons in even the brief mentions of many of the women of the Bible.

The point is that if we're interested in presenting a comprehensive and balanced view of God's Kingdom, we will look for, study, and teach the stories of the women as well as the men.

More than fifteen years ago, I (Scot) wrote a book called *The Jesus Creed*, which included a chapter on Mary, the mother of Jesus. In that chapter, I told other stories about women as well.

Not long after the book came out, a male church leader called me to say two things: first, he liked the book; and second, because the stories in that chapter were about women, he couldn't relate to them. My response? "How do you think the women and girls in your church feel *every* Sunday?"

Second, a church marked by a culture of *tov*, empathy, and compassion will *know the names and stories of women in church history*. Before you turn the page and move on, make a note to go to your favorite bookstore, or take a minute right now to visit your favorite site on the Internet for purchasing books and buy a copy of Ruth Tucker's *Extraordinary Women of Church History*. When it lands in your lap, start reading it and telling others about women in the history of the church, women like Mary McLeod Bethune.

Mary McLeod Bethune was the first African American woman to establish a four-year college. She was the first African American to hold a high-level government directorship.[13] She advised three American presidents and was "arguably the most powerful African American person in the United States" between 1933 and 1945, according to one of her biographers.[14] Her focus was on evangelism, education, and social reform. At Bethune College (now Bethune-Cookman), her curriculum was Bible, Industry, and English.

In 1936, she reflected on her life and how Christianity worked in the US:

> The Negro must go to a separate church even though he claims to be of the same denomination [as some whites]. He is not allowed to sing, in unison with the white man, the grand old hymns of Calvin, the Wesleys—the triumphant songs of Christ and eternal glory. When at last he is called to his final resting place on earth even his ashes are not allowed to mingle with those of his white

brother, but are borne away to some remote place where the white man is not even reminded that this Negro ever lived. Judging from all that has preceded the Negro in death, it looks as if he has been prepared for a heaven separate from the one to which the white man feels he alone is fit to inhabit.[15]

She experienced the utter violation of dignity that white folks used against African Americans, but that didn't stop her. She reversed the thunder of racism by conquering her enemies with love, with industry, with strategy, and with an educational system designed for the "uplift" of women and African Americans.

We know the story of Martin Luther King Jr., but the life of this prominent and influential woman is all but forgotten. In a *tov* culture, inequities like this will be addressed and rectified as we seek to discover and celebrate heroes of the faith from all corners of the church.

Two of the greatest theologians in the history of the church were Saint Basil the Great and his brother Gregory of Nyssa. Along with their friend Gregory of Nazianzus, they became known as the Cappadocian Fathers, and in the early fourth century they framed what is now called Christian Orthodoxy.

Their stories and their theology are well known, but the same cannot be said for their brilliant, godly, and exemplary sister, Macrina. When her fiancé died, she chose not to marry another and lived as an ascetic nun instead. She was a brilliant theologian in her own right, as her brothers openly acknowledged; she founded a monastery and lived her life utterly dedicated to God— in prayer, in study, in conversation, and in works of *tov*. Yet very few outside the Orthodox tradition know her name. It's time we started telling the stories of women like Macrina, as well.

In 2018, John Piper, one of America's more influential pastors and authors, wrote a book called *21 Servants of Sovereign Joy*, focusing on the lives of spiritual giants in the history of the church. But his collection only includes twenty-one white men— no women, no people of color. In the Circle of *Tov*, we need to expand our reach to include the stories of women and minorities. How else can we represent and begin to understand the scope and diversity of Christ's body on earth?

Third, a congregation dedicated to fostering a culture of *tov* will *know the names and stories of women in their own local church history.* Why? Because we need to see our common history through the eyes of women so we can begin to honor and value their contributions.

Fourth, a *tov* church culture *nurtures women as agents of God's redemptive work in the world.* To encourage and acknowledge and celebrate the lesser-known contributors to the life of the church, we need to incorporate stories of women, of marginalized or wounded people, into our sermons. I (Scot) know how hard this is because I have preached many sermons without expanding the circle of recognition. Even when I have committed to incorporating women or minorities or the marginalized into my sermons, I have had trouble finding stories—because so often they haven't been told. But I can depend on my dear wife, Kris, to remind me every time I preach a non-inclusive sermon. And she takes note of this deficiency at conferences, as well. We need such people, who will be the conscience of the congregation, who will continually encourage inclusivity and expanding the Circle of *Tov*.

Telling the stories of women and other marginalized groups boosts their visibility and affirms their gifts—and it encourages others in the congregation to do the same. It nurtures a culture of empathy for women, for the hurting, for the downtrodden. Every church leader needs to ask if they are nurturing the gifts of *everyone* in their congregation.

Fifth, a church with a *tov* culture will *intentionally promote the contributions of women on the church's webpage and on the platform during services.* Everyone knows the power of advertising to both establish and maintain a desired mindset. Give women a platform; tell their stories from the pulpit, on the webpage, and in your church's social media. This highlighting of the contributions of women will both affirm them and nurture a culture that will continue to honor and value women. A culture that is empathetic to women and the marginalized will stifle a culture of narcissism.

When a male-based culture is re-formed into a male-and-female-based culture, it presents a truer picture of the character of God, who created *all* people as his image bearers. When the voices of women become customary, common, expected, and accepted, the church becomes more inviting, more inclusive, more empathetic, more compassionate, safer, and more secure—for everyone. We pray for that day.

TOV CHURCHES NURTURE GRACE

PASTORS SHAPED BY GOODNESS are grace dispensers, agents of God called to help, be with, and offer grace to those whom they are called to serve. Pastor Harold Senkbeil is a longtime Lutheran pastor who grew up on a farm and learned some of life's most pastoral lessons from his farmer father. One of those lessons was tender grace. Roberta (not her real name) was on her deathbed with cancer when Pastor Senkbeil attended to her and ministered the grace of *tov*. Every *tov* pastor I know tells of similar experiences to this one:

> Roberta's cancer was a particularly nasty variety; by
> now it had eaten its way into most of her vital organs.
> The scarf that concealed her balding head bore silent
> testimony to the radical regimen of chemotherapy her
> body had endured in a vain attempt to stave off death.

She extended a weak hand and a wan smile to greet her
pastor. Her skin was pasty and cold to the touch, her
breaths labored and shallow, exuding the sweetly sour
smell of impending death. Though her eyes were losing
their luster, she gladly, eagerly heard the word of God,
clinging to every syllable. "Would you like the Lord's
Supper?" I asked. "Oh yes," she whispered.

As he offered her the bread and the wine, tokens of God's
grace, he quickly realized the logistical challenge presented by her
physical weakness.

How to commune someone who could no longer lift
her head? Gingerly slipping onto the edge of her bed, I
gently wrapped one arm beneath her frail, bony shoulders
and lifted her feather-light torso, cradling her like some
skeletal baby. With my other hand I placed in her mouth
the gifts her Savior died to bring: the bread of heaven here
on earth, the cup of salvation poured out for all the world.
"Take, eat, the body of Christ, given for you," I said.
"Take, drink, his blood shed for you for the forgiveness
of your sins." Then a parting blessing with the sign of the
cross traced on her ashen forehead with my thumb: "The
body and blood of our Lord Jesus Christ strengthen and
preserve you in body and in soul unto life everlasting.
Depart in his peace."
    And she did. Not right then, but not many days
later. . . .
    That day there in Roberta's apartment, as I packed
up my communion case and bade farewell to her family
and friends keeping vigil with her, one of them said
admiringly: "You had death in your hands here today."

I'm not sure how I responded then. But here's what I should have said: "Maybe so, but I also had life in my hands to bring."[1]

Exactly. What the *tov* church has to offer is the grace that brings life to others. How can a pastor who offers the grace of the body and blood of Jesus then turn around and abuse women, blister staff members with verbal shaming, or exploit the people he is called to serve? It makes no sense. Any church that deforms into a power-based, fear-inducing, exploitative culture no longer offers the grace of life, but rather the bones of death. To resist such a toxic culture, we must understand how to build and sustain a life-giving culture of grace.

THE CIRCLE OF *TOV*
Nurturing Habits of Goodness

TOV

Nurture empathy
Resist a narcissist's culture

Nurture grace
Resist a fear culture

SEVEN FEATURES OF A GRACE-FILLED CULTURE

Read this definition slowly: Grace-filled goodness begins in forgiveness, forms into freedom, and resists fear—all because it knows that God's design for the church is love. The apostle John captures it perfectly in his first letter:

> There is no fear in love. But perfect love drives out fear, because fear has to do with punishment. The one who fears is not made perfect in love.[2]

In the words of New Testament scholar John M. G. Barclay, "'Grace' is a multi-faceted concept best approached through the category of gift. . . . 'Gift' denotes the sphere of voluntary, personal relations, characterized by goodwill in the giving of benefit or favor, and eliciting some form of reciprocal return that is both voluntary and necessary for the continuation of the relationship."[3]

Here is how a gift- or grace-filled culture works.

First, *someone has something to give.* In this case, the giver is God and the gift is redemption. Grace is not something we deserve or can earn based on status or achievement. In a grace-based culture, habits of giving are noticeable because we know we ourselves are the recipients of God's gift of grace.

Second, *our tov God decides to give us this redemption.* At the heart of redemption is *forgiveness*, a term that is illustrated by a couple of wonderful images in the Bible. At times, sin is seen as a *burden* we bear, like a rock-filled backpack we are just barely able to carry that brings constant irritation and overbearing weight. Forgiveness enables us to drop the burden or have God take the burden and throw it away. At other times, forgiveness is likened to *canceling a debt.* Imagine here a credit card debt that goes well beyond our income, and the rapidly accruing interest is a constant reminder that we may never have enough funds to pay it off. Paul tells us that God abolished our indebtedness at the cross: "He canceled the record of the charges against us and took it away by nailing it to the cross."[4] In a church called *tov*, when grace forms the culture, forgiveness flows freely between God and his people and between one person and another. When a power-and-fear-based culture develops, grace is soon abandoned and forgiveness all but forgotten.

Third, *the giving and receiving of the gift of grace creates a bond*, a personal relationship between the giver (God) and the receiver (us). It also creates a bond between people in the church as they give grace to others and others receive it. In short order, relational bonds of reciprocal grace form and begin to function.

Fourth, *the receiver responds with action*. When the fundamental response to God's gift of grace is thankfulness, the receiver will reciprocate with active expressions of gratitude, praise and worship, love and obedience, trust and service. The entirety of the Christian life is a response to the gift of grace our *tov* God has given us.

Fifth, *our gift-giving God becomes the Father of a multitude of brothers and sisters*. This observation requires more extensive discussion because it is the foundation for the establishment of a grace culture. We become a gift-based family of grace givers and receivers—not just the pastors or leaders, but every one of us. The gift of grace does not establish a hierarchy of power relationships, in which some people are deemed superior to others. It makes us all siblings of one another. The gracious gift of God's *tov* makes us all equally loved and valued members of the body of Christ.

It bears repeating: In the church, no one is greater than another. Jesus Christ alone is the head. Just as no one merits inclusion in this new family of siblings, no sister is more of a sister than any other sister, and no brother is more of a brother than any other brother. Everyone is a sibling, and siblings have equal status. Moreover, no brother or sister becomes a "father" or a "mother." There is—to quote Jesus—only one Father.[5]

True sibling equality has huge implications for ending power-based and fear-inducing cultures. Equality under God the Father and Christ his Son wipes out any hierarchy of superiority and rank. The term *brothers and sisters* reinforces the truth that we are "all one in Christ Jesus."[6]

Sixth, *grace is a reverse kind of power that turns our siblingship into a flourishing family reality.* The gift of grace transforms us from enemies of God and strangers to one another into members of one big, grace-filled family. Unleashing grace has the power to form us into a people who love one another to a degree we never thought possible.

Seventh, *the Holy Spirit is the active agent who turns us from enemies and strangers into friends and family.* We cannot do this on our own; we have neither the capacity nor the ability. One of my favorite lines comes from New Testament scholar James D. G. Dunn, who once said that the Holy Spirit "transcends human ability and transforms human inability."[7]

Let's dwell on this for a moment: We are not capable of forming our churches into grace-filled, people-first *tov* cultures. Rather, we bring an assortment of inabilities and incompatibilities. For example, some of us are introverts and others are aggressive extroverts, and thus we don't mix well. We come from different ethnicities, and we don't trust each other. As males and females, we don't always understand or appreciate one another. We love status and hierarchy and power, and we struggle with treating one another with grace and love. Yes, we have an assortment of abilities as well, but we still need the Holy Spirit to transcend those abilities and transform us into a flourishing family filled with people-first people and givers of grace.

REQUIREMENTS FOR A
GRACE-SHAPED CHURCH CULTURE

Nothing is clearer in the missionary work of the apostle Paul than his determination to not only get people saved, but to get saved people to learn how to get along with one another. Particularly those who had not traveled in the same circles. His mission, it can be said, was to expand the close-knit nation of Israel into a multiethnic people. In hindsight, Paul might want to adapt a well-known line from C. S. Lewis, who said, "Everyone says forgiveness is a lovely idea until he has something to forgive."[8] Likewise, we might say that merging disparate people into the family of God is a lovely idea until you try to do it.

Not surprisingly, creating a grace-based family of siblings requires *trust*, the invisible glue that binds people together. Power and fear can undermine trust, but grace creates it. Without trust, there can be no genuine siblingship. To trust someone is to believe in that person in ways that make the world safe. Sadly, in fear-based power cultures, trust breaks down and makes life as siblings nearly impossible. When a collection of siblings called a church has untrusting relationships, the family breaks down into cliques and tribes and interest groups.

Trusting relationships are built on *reciprocity*—we must give in order to get. As one sibling contributes to the family and another receives that gift, a society of reciprocity is formed—a mutual gift-exchange. That is what a church is. Power-based and fear-inducing church cultures are one-way streets: The flow of trust is toward the pastor, the leaders, the powerful. But in a grace-based church, reciprocity flows freely, as do the gifts.

Building our theme point by point: When siblings all see themselves as receivers of God's gift, when we allow ourselves to be transformed by God's grace into equal participants who love and trust one another, nothing less than a grace-based culture of *freedom* will be formed.

In the Bible, freedom is both a freedom *from* (sin in all its hideous expressions) and a freedom *for* (becoming the children and siblings that God designed and desires). Freedom creates trust just as trust creates freedom. Again, reciprocity.

A fear-based culture stifles freedom through legalism, authoritarianism, status, and approval-based relationships. That's not freedom, and that's not love. "Perfect love drives out fear."[9] When fear prevails in a church, there is no real love.

One last element in a grace-shaped church culture is *space* or *room*—room to learn and make mistakes, room for growth and for forgiveness. In a fear-inducing power culture, mistakes can prompt verbal abuse and lead to status degradation or public shaming. Fear can overwhelm or undermine the Christian virtue of forgiveness. In a grace-shaped culture, space is allowed for siblings to discover their giftedness and calling, space (and grace) is allowed for siblings to make mistakes as they grow in their giftedness, and there is space to forgive others for their mistakes. Persistent acts of grace create a *tov* culture filled with grace.

TOV CHURCHES NURTURE A PEOPLE-FIRST CULTURE

IN THE CIRCLE OF *TOV*, we find churches that nurture empathy, compassion, and grace. These values in turn become the foundation for nurturing a *people-first* culture in the church. A church that puts people first will *resist* the notion of the church primarily as an institution.

Seeing church primarily as an institution creates a culture in which empathy, compassion, and grace can be pushed aside in the interests of a particular theology or set of convictions. The church may not do this intentionally, but as any organization grows, there is a tendency toward "institution creep," in which the needs of the organization—which may be coldhearted, misdirected, and anything but grace-filled—begin to supersede the needs of the *people* in the organization. That's when people get squashed.

Church as an institution can become coercive, but a people-first church will treat people with the highest degree of dignity, respect, and integrity.

THE CIRCLE OF *TOV*
Nurturing Habits of Goodness

TOV

Nurture empathy
Resist a narcissist's culture

Nurture grace
Resist a fear culture

Put people first
Resist institution creep

Perhaps no one in recent memory exemplifies a people-first perspective and the virtues of dignity, respect, and integrity more than Fred Rogers. That's right, everyone's friend from *Mister Rogers' Neighborhood.* He created a culture of *tov* in the arena of broadcast television, an environment one would have to think is far more difficult than inside the church. And yet he maintained that goodness culture for more than three decades, even as the social mores in American culture shifted all around him.

Fred Rogers was bullied as a youngster and excluded from the crowd, so he grew up with an empathetic understanding of what it feels like to be the underdog and to struggle to fit in. As an adult, he combined his training in ministry, music, and child development with his Christian faith and family-taught virtues of generosity, kindness, tolerance, and empathy to create a unique television program that focused on the emotional, moral, spiritual, and intellectual life of children.

Speaking before the United States Congress, Fred Rogers explained his mission:

> I give an expression of care every day to each child, to help him realize that he is unique. I end the program by saying, "You've made this day a special day, by just your being you. There's no person in the whole world like you, and I like you, just the way you are."[1]

Maxwell King in his biography of Fred Rogers, *The Good Neighbor*, describes the strong sense of self-discipline at the heart of Mr. Rogers's life:

> Fred Rogers got up every morning between 4:30 and 5:30 a.m. to read the Bible and prepare himself for the day before he went to the Pittsburgh Athletic Association to swim. But Rogers's preparation was not so much professional as it was spiritual: He would study passages of interest from the Bible, and then he would visualize who he would be seeing that day, so that he would be prepared to be as caring and giving as he could be. Fred's prayers in those early morning sessions were not for success or accomplishment, but rather for the goodness of heart to be the best person he could be in each of the encounters he would have that day.[2]

Many who knew Fred Rogers said he was the same person behind closed doors and in the studio as he was on-screen. There was no duplicity in his character. Tom Junod, a notoriously hard-nosed interviewer from *Esquire* magazine who often dented and even crushed the reputation of well-known stars, had this to say about Mister Rogers: "What was amazing about Fred was that he was the exact same person he was on TV. There was no show, no act—that was him."[3] Elizabeth Seamans, who worked with Rogers for years, said, "He was not proud or arrogant. He didn't take anything or anybody for granted, ever. He was flawed, but he was a really, really great man, and a good man."[4]

It might be tempting to look at Mister Rogers as an outlier because his persona is so distinctive, so countercultural, and even unexpected. But what set Fred Roger apart is not beyond our reach. As Maxwell King observes, "Fred Rogers never—ever—let the urgency of work or life impede his focus on what he saw as basic human values: integrity, respect, responsibility, fairness and compassion, and . . . kindness."[5] In other words, *people first*. He simply put *tov* into practice and stubbornly, consistently stayed with it. Certainly that avenue is open to all of us.

Tov always takes root first in the hearts of individuals, who then work together with like-minded others to create a goodness culture.

BECOMING A PEOPLE-FIRST CHURCH

In August 2019, Mitch Randall, an ordained Southern Baptist pastor and the executive director of EthicsDaily.com, exhorted the church to align itself with the wisdom of the workplace, where various forms of malpractice are named. Randall wanted to create a definition of *theological* malpractice. One of his main points addresses the issue of people vs. institutions and policies:

Beliefs that place more value on the institution of the
church over the humanity of victims misses the central
teaching of the gospel. In other words, when loving God
and neighbor falls by the wayside to the preservation of
institutional and professional reputations, then that, by
definition, is theological malpractice."[6]

Exactly! A goodness culture seeks to conform our lives to Christ's
example, by focusing on people instead of institutions.

Randall defines theological malpractice as "the perversion of
the gospel, based upon a flawed hermeneutical philosophy built
upon patriarchalism and misogyny that protects the reputations of
clergy, churches, denominations, and institutions and debases the
rights of victims, causing physical, mental, emotional and spiritual
damage."[7] In plain terms, theological malpractice can be summarized in the following points:

1. It perverts the gospel of *tov*.
2. It begins in male-centeredness and fosters anti-female
   attitudes.
3. It protects the institution at the expense of people.
4. It protects the leaders of the institution.
5. It violates human rights.
6. It damages people.

At the heart of theological malpractice is a failure to treat all
people as God's image-bearers—which strikes at the heart of our
Christian faith.

So, what can we do to resist institution creep and theological
malpractice? What can we do to regain a people-first culture in
our churches? We'd like to suggest five essential practices: (1) treat

people as people, (2) enfold others into the community, (3) recognize all people as made in the image of God, (4) treat people as siblings, and (5) develop Jesus-like eyes for people.

Treat people as people

Allow me (Scot) to give a personal example. Our whole family sits together at church—Kris and me, Laura and Mark, Lukas and Annika with Aksel and Finley. In front of us are Lesley and Gil, often Paula and Kristin, sometimes Roger, sometimes April. At the end of our row are Kris's sister Pat and sometimes Laurie. Nearby are Alice, an eightysomething retired seminary professor and dean, and her husband, ninetysomething Randy, a former missionary and pastor who seems to know the name of everyone in the entire church and often tells us he's been praying for us. When Kris and I have to miss a Sunday due to travel or speaking, Randy always tells me he'll be praying for us. When Randy and Alice missed two weeks in a row, I was able to assure Rosalie, yet another regular, that they were on a trip to see family. I could go on about the vital people-connections in our congregation, but you get the idea.

For our family, church is all about the people. I don't know what our attendance numbers are per week. Sometimes the room is full and sometimes not. Children bustle about and sometimes it's noisy, but children are noisy and people are bustlers. When the children leave the central worship for their own classrooms, it's like a parade, and it seems to draw a smile from all the adults. These kids are growing up before our eyes. Most everyone seems to know everyone else. When Kris and I are away for a Sunday, we miss specific people—such as Ethan, with whom I may have wanted to talk about Flannery O'Connor or Willa Cather. Or Andrew, or Laurie, or Otto, or Elana and Anthony and their son Eli.

We're not saying that small is beautiful and big is bad. We don't believe that. Some megachurches comprise hundreds of small groups or house churches that meet on Sunday or once a month. Some megachurches have worked hard to form a people-first ministry by encouraging everyone to participate in small groups where they can get to know others and be known. Still, we can acknowledge that megachurches will have to be more *intentional* about creating a people-first culture or the ethos of the church can quickly become a "come hear me preach" or "come hear the music" culture.

The Circle of *Tov* begins when a church sees people as people and treats them as people by nurturing them to become what God designed them to be. People with names and histories and stories. People who are doing well and people who are not. People who are recovering from church abuse. People who've had surgeries and sicknesses. People who are aging. People who are rich and poor and everything in between. People who are wounded and in need of healing, people who are unemployed and underemployed, people who need encouragement or tangible assistance. The essence of treating people as people can be summed up in twelve simple words from Jesus: "Do to others as you would like them to do to you."[8]

Enfold others into the community

It's simple enough to think of the church as people, but sometimes it's a challenge to give the idea full play. Those people are not living in isolation; they are living in relationship. And relationship is all about *belonging*.

Whether people will admit it or not, everyone wants to belong. Everyone wants to feel valued. At the heart of a people-first church culture will always be a commitment to enfold others into the community. That starts with building relationships: learning people's names, encouraging them to tell their story, sharing your story with them, including them in the life of the church family (both inside and outside the walls of the church building), inviting them to become a part of the church community.

Enfolding others into community could mean welcoming them into your home and eating with them. Here's an example of a couple, Kathy Fletcher and David Simpson, who became agents of *tov* by opening up their dinner table.

Kathy and David's son, who attended a public school in Washington, DC, had some friends who came from poor families. So he started inviting them over. One friend invited some of his other poor friends, and before long more than two dozen kids were coming for dinner each week. Soon, other adults were coming as well, and the table of generosity became a table of healing for all.[9]

Bill Milliken, founder of Communities in Schools, an organization working to bring community resources inside the public schools, came to the table one night. When he saw the relationships that Kathy Fletcher and David Simpson had built, and all they were doing, he said, "I've been working in this field for fifty years . . . and I've never seen a program turn around a life. Only relationships turn around lives."[10] Elsewhere, he remarked, "A great program simply creates the environment for healthy relationships to form."[11]

Relationship building takes time, and it takes time for people to become fully integrated into a genuine Circle of *Tov* in a church. Over time, we learn one another's names; over time, we learn one another's stories; over time, we tell our own stories; over time, we become true siblings in Christ; over time, we learn one another's ways and learn to consider one another in our decisions. It takes time for a group of strangers to become a family. But once we get to this level of commitment, we can't *not* treat people as people.

That also means we will *see* when they are not being treated as people by others.

Recognize all people as made in the image of God

As Christians, we know that God designed every person to be his image bearer: "Let us," God says, "make human beings in our image, to be like us."[12] Another translation reads, "Let us make mankind in our image, in our likeness."[13] Along with our design comes a statement of purpose—that we will "reign over" what God has created. Our role as image bearers is to subgovern God's world on God's behalf. That is the mission for each and every one of us.

What does it mean to be an image bearer? The apostle Paul says this about Jesus: "Christ is the visible image of the invisible God."[14] In other words, Jesus Christ is the *one true image* of God. This also means that when God created humans, his template was Jesus. And here's the best *tov* news of all: We are being transformed from our sinfulness into the very image of Christ. Paul establishes this truth three times in three different ways, so we will be certain to take notice:

- Romans 8:29: "God knew his people in advance, and he chose them to become like his Son,"[15] or "conformed to the image of his Son."[16]
- 2 Corinthians 3:18: "All of us who have had that veil removed can see and reflect the glory of the Lord. And the Lord—who is the Spirit—makes us more and more like him as we are changed into his glorious image."
- 2 Corinthians 4:4: "Those who don't believe . . . are unable to see the glorious light of the Good News. They don't understand this message about the glory of Christ, who is the exact likeness of God."

Here's why we treat people as people and not as "giving units." Each person we meet is designed by God to look like Christ. As such, we are to give everyone profound respect and honor for *who they are*—even if the image of God in them has been tarnished or "painted over" by sinful choices. Recognizing all people as made in the image of God means always seeing their *potential*, not just their present sinful condition. As Paul said to the Corinthians, "Some of you were once like that. But you were cleansed; you were made holy; you were made right with God by calling on the name of the Lord Jesus Christ and by the Spirit of our God."[17] I've been impressed again and again by Paul's courage to say this about—of all people—the Corinthians!

A goodness culture will always confront sin as sin. (We'll look more closely at this in a later chapter about telling the truth and nurturing a culture of truth.) And a goodness culture will always seek to move people toward true repentance. But even as we confront sin in the church, we don't want to lose sight of the *glorious image of God* inherent in each and every person.

Treat people as siblings

The most common word in the New Testament for Christian believers—by far—is not *church*; it is *siblings* or *brothers and sisters*. When Paul sent the runaway slave Onesimus back to his owner, Philemon, he told Philemon to welcome Onesimus back "no longer as a slave, but better than a slave, as a dear *brother*."[18] The desired outcome of treating other people as people is to begin to see them as brothers or sisters.

Paul's vision was remarkably progressive for his day: Within the body of Christ, he says, we are to consider one another no longer according to social status, ethnic status, or gendered status. "There is no longer Jew or Gentile, slave or free, male and female. For you are all one in Christ Jesus."[19] That is, we are all siblings.

The essence of a family is relationships, and the foundation of our relationships in the Circle of *Tov* is that we are siblings united in Christ. In a goodness culture, we are to honor one another as people because we know who we are (image bearers of God) and who we belong to. We are brothers and sisters in Christ.

To nurture a culture of *tov*, we must resist whatever does not treat people as siblings.

So how *do* we treat siblings?

Perhaps you grew up without any siblings, or maybe you didn't have such a great relationship with your siblings. But what we're talking about here is how siblings interact in a healthy family environment. At the very least, the following will be true:

Siblings care about one another.
Siblings look out for one another.
Siblings protect one another.
Siblings believe one another.
Siblings trust one another.
Siblings see the good and the bad and love each other
    anyway.

Churches with a goodness culture will do what is right because they love people and want only the best for them.

Develop Jesus-like eyes for people

When Jesus looked at people, he saw past outward appearances and went straight to the heart; he looked beyond the posturing and self-protective facades and zeroed in on their real needs. The Gospels often use the word *compassion*—a word that means commiseration, showing pity, and being filled with mercy— to describe Jesus' outlook on people.[20] The word *compassion* describes an inner organ turning in pain when it sees human suffering. How did the Gospel writers and apostles know that Jesus was filled with compassion? There are only three options: he told them, his face showed it, or his tears flowed. Two and three are the most likely. However, Jesus' emotional response to those in need was not simply to "feel bad" about their circumstances; it was an emotional response that prompted *action*. Each time the Gospel writers describe the compassion of Jesus, they also tell us what he *did*: he healed, he cured, he cleansed, he taught, he pastored.

The apostle Paul had a similar heart for people—though many people today get him wrong on this one. They think of Paul as a power-mongering, workaholic, money-grubbing, anti-woman, proslavery authoritarian who gathered together groups of new Christians and set up some rules for them before pushing off the for next shore, and who heard some stories about nonsense in those gatherings and dashed off angry letters telling everyone how to live. Okay, that's an overstatement, but not by much, if you've ever heard the critiques of Christianity offered by some people today. Now read 2 Corinthians 2:12-13 and ask yourself if it lines up with the critical view of Paul mentioned above.

> When I came to the city of Troas to preach the Good News of Christ, the Lord opened a door of opportunity for me. But I had no peace of mind because my dear brother Titus hadn't yet arrived with a report from you. So I said good-bye and went on to Macedonia to find him.

Here's a man who had such an intense love for the Corinthians (who, at least in Paul's mind, lacked that same love for him) and concern for his protégé Titus that he stopped in his tracks and couldn't go on until he saw Titus and heard about the welfare of the Corinthians. Paula Gooder, chancellor of St. Paul's Cathedral in London, puts it this way: "Paul—the greatest evangelist of all time—passed up the opportunity to preach the gospel because his friend Titus was not there."[21] And not just "his friend," but his "dear brother." People first.

Notice now the focus of Paul's mission to the church in Colossae—which was almost entirely a group of people he'd never met! We've italicized the people-oriented words:

> *We* tell *others* about Christ, warning *everyone* and teaching *everyone* with all the wisdom God has given *us*. *We* want to present *them* to God, perfect in *their* relationship to Christ. That's why *I* work and struggle so hard, depending on Christ's mighty power that works within *me*. *I* want *you* to know how much *I* have agonized for *you* and for *the church* at Laodicea, and for many other *believers* who have never met *me* personally. *I* want *them* to be encouraged and knit together by strong ties of love. *I* want *them* to have complete confidence that *they* understand God's mysterious plan, which is Christ himself.[22]

Agonizing, encouraging, knitting together with "strong ties of love." Paul was nothing if not compassionate and people-first. It was the foundation of his entire ministry.

Beliefs and behaviors are all about belonging to one another. The vision of the New Testament turns us *away* from individualism and *toward* committed relationships with other people. The Bible's vision of *tov* is all about people in relationship with others. It's about people being *good* (*tov*) to one another. A people-first culture instinctively treats people as image bearers and as siblings.

Relationships in the Circle of *Tov* are shaped by one of the

Bible's most beautiful words: *truth*. Truth is so central to *tov* that we will devote the next chapter to unfolding its meaning. Because truth telling is where toxic church cultures always fail, we need to take a close look at the subject.

TOV CHURCHES NURTURE TRUTH

IF YOU WANT TO HEAR THE BRUTAL TRUTH about yourself, step into a bustling classroom of first graders. Every day, they nonchalantly but oh-so-honestly tell me (Laura) things like these:

"Mrs. Barringer, you have something green on your tooth."
"You look tired today, Mrs. Barringer."
"I liked your hair better yesterday."
"You make no sense."
"Why is your face shiny?"
"I can tell you're not really blonde, Mrs. Barringer."
"Your eyes look different. ARE YOU NOT WEARING MAKEUP?"

And every woman's favorite:

"Do you have a baby in your stomach, Mrs. Barringer?" (No.)

My first graders tell me the detailed truth of their home happenings, as well:

"My dad likes beer. A lot."
"My mom is a lot older than my dad."
"Our neighbors call the cops on us all the time."

But here's the thing: I never have to wonder what my first graders are thinking. They tell me the truth about myself, about themselves, and about their family life, and I don't even have to ask. Every day, they offer direct, unsolicited, immediate feedback:

"That story wasn't very good."
"You should stop talking so we can get on with our work."

Kids are natural truth tellers. We have much to learn from the natural truth-telling tendencies of young children. Could truth telling be part of what Jesus meant when he said, "Truly I tell you, unless you change and become like little children, you will never enter the kingdom of heaven"?[1]

FORMING A TRUTH-TELLING CULTURE

The Bible calls us to know the truth, tell the truth, and live in the truth. Not only that, but we profess that our faith *is* the truth. Truth is one of the New Testament writers' favorite words to describe Jesus, the gospel, salvation, and the Christian way of life. Paul tells us that "God our Savior . . . wants everyone to be saved and to understand the truth."[2] Later, Paul adds that "the church of the living God . . . is the pillar and foundation of the truth."[3]

So if God is the truth, our faith is the truth, and we are to walk in the truth, anything that opposes the truth or undermines the truth is not of God and not part of a truth-telling *tov* culture. There is no room in a church called *tov* for lying, deceit, cover-ups, suppression, gaslighting, or spin. All those things are toxic.

Telling the truth, then, is *who we are* as Christians. When we don't tell the truth, we deny our *identity* and our *calling*.

So, what is required to form a truth-telling culture? A culture of truth telling can only be formed through the disciplines of knowing the truth, doing the truth, and surrendering to the truth. Truth telling also requires us to *resist* what is false and to fight anything that is less than truthful. We must emphasize the importance of truth, because too many churches are falling short of the mark.

THE CIRCLE OF *TOV*
Nurturing Habits of Goodness

Nurture empathy
Resist a narcissist's culture

TOV

Nurture grace
Resist a fear culture

Put people first
Resist institution creep

Tell the truth
Resist false narratives
Know Yom Kippur
Form a truth-telling culture

KNOWING THE TRUTH

If we want to create a truth-telling culture, we first must discern *what the truth is.* Christianity make an astonishing claim that truth is not merely an ideal or a set of ideas or a philosophy; instead, truth is *embodied* in the person of Jesus Christ. The Gospel of John tells us that "we have seen . . . the glory of the one and only Son, who came from the Father, *full of grace and truth*."[4] Jesus said of himself, "I am the way, *the truth*, and the life. No one can come to the Father except through me."[5]

Sometimes it's easier to quote Bible verses than to absorb the truth of them, but we cannot overlook this foundational truth about our faith: God is revealed in Jesus Christ, so that how he lives, what he teaches, and what he does are the *only* true measures for truth.

C. S. Lewis offers a lovely illustration of how the truth about Jesus as the highest measure of good penetrates to the level of the soul. In his novel *The Lion, the Witch and the Wardrobe*, he writes:

> Signaling to the children to stand as close around it as they possibly could, . . . [the Beaver] added in a low whisper—
>
> "They say Aslan is on the move—perhaps has already landed."
>
> And now a very curious thing happened. None of the children knew who Aslan was any more than you do; but the moment the Beaver had spoken these words everyone felt quite different. Perhaps it has sometimes happened to you in a dream that someone says something which you don't understand but in the dream it feels as if it had some enormous meaning—either a terrifying one which

turns the whole dream into a nightmare or else a lovely
meaning too lovely to put into words, which makes the
dream so beautiful that you remember it all your life and
are always wishing you could get into that dream again.
It was like that now. At the name of Aslan each one of the
children felt something jump in its inside. Edmund felt a
sensation of mysterious horror. Peter felt suddenly brave
and adventurous. Susan felt as if some delicious smell or
some delightful strain of music had just floated by her.
And Lucy got the feeling you have when you wake up in
the morning and realize it is the beginning of the holidays
or the beginning of summer.[6]

Okay, you might say, I'm with you. I believe Jesus is the truth.
And we are to live in the truth—I believe that, as well. But how
can we *know* the truth? Jesus answers this question for us in John
15–16 when he foretells the coming of the Holy Spirit, whom he
calls "the Spirit of truth," who "will guide you into all truth."[7] And
regarding the revelation of Jesus as God's Son "by his baptism in
water and by shedding his blood on the cross," the Holy Spirit,
"who is truth, confirms it with his testimony."[8] So it is by the power
of the Holy Spirit that we can know and learn the truth. It is also
by the power of the Spirit that we are able to *do* the truth.

DOING THE TRUTH

Because Jesus is the truth, if he dwells in us and we dwell in him,
truth becomes our way of life. And along with truth comes love,
for love "rejoices with the truth."[9] We take joy in the truth, and we
are saddened when the truth is not told. "As servants of God," Paul
writes, "we commend ourselves . . . in truthful speech."[10] Paul also
says, "Each of you must put off falsehood and speak truthfully to

your neighbor."[11] And he exhorts us, "Stand firm . . . with the belt of truth buckled around your waist."[12]

The way of Christian living, then, is all about truth telling. The apostle John paints this idea with bold colors when he writes, "If we claim to have fellowship with [God] and yet walk in the darkness, we lie and do not live out the truth."[13] Walking in darkness is the opposite of truth telling. Likewise, when a church chooses false narratives to obscure the truth, they are choosing darkness over light, and lies over the truth.

Miroslav Volf, America's most public theological intellectual, and his associate Matthew Croasmun have written a wonderful book called *For the Life of the World*, in which they connect truth with Christian character: "Truth seeking is a constitutive dimension of living the true life; and living the true life . . . is a condition of the search for its truthful articulation."[14] Simply stated, followers of Jesus are to be truth tellers. Likewise, a truth-telling culture emerges from people who live in the truth, and living in the truth fosters people who tell the truth. Life and speech—living a true life and telling the truth—are vitally connected.

SURRENDERING TO THE TRUTH

Truth telling is not always easy. When Vonda Dyer agreed to share her story with the *Chicago Tribune* in 2018, she had no idea of the personal turmoil that would result. In September 2019, she told her story at the No More Silence conference at Dallas Theological Seminary:

> I did not want to come forward. I did not want to be
> the one to speak. But for the sake of the purity and the
> integrity of the church that I love . . . I soon realized that I
> would need to have courage to speak up, even if it meant

losing everything. Some days it feels as though I almost have. Coming forward was the hardest, most challenging, painful, life-altering decision I have ever had to make. What it has cost me is immeasurable. I had no idea that the church that I loved would not believe me and the nine other women as claims mounted. I had no idea that the church would continue to believe the pastor in question, even though years of allegations had been swirling and brought to their attention with no action taken. I did not imagine they would assassinate my character publicly. I was naive and could not imagine being persecuted, slandered, lied about, and continually bullied by the church on a global scale for reasons I may never fully know. I did not know how crushing it would be to come forward.[15]

A truth-telling culture calls us to *surrender* to the truth—to be humble and vulnerable and willing to submit ourselves to the truth even when it's most difficult. God summons us toward the light because he *is* the light and he wants us to live in "the true light that gives light to everyone."[16] Notice these words from Jesus, who knew the human heart better than anyone: "Those who do what is right come to the light so others can see that they are doing what God wants."[17] God's call for us to live in the true light is an exhortation to know the truth, make truth a way of life, open ourselves to the Spirit's revealing truth, and be vulnerable to the truth so that we can live honestly before God.

ONLY THE TRUTH HEALS AND SETS US FREE

In the heart of the Circle of *Tov* there is a saving, healing, restorative power unlike anything we can discover in any other way.

Truth is a person; that person speaks truth to us, and his spoken word heals us. The Bible describes the wonderful work of God in many ways: God saves, God rescues, God ransoms, God heals, God cures, and God reconciles. Jesus said it this way: "You will know the truth, and the truth will set you free."[18]

In a culture of *tov*, truth prevails because God's people choose to live in the light of God's truth. Living in the light sets us free to love the light and hate the darkness. It also motivates us to shine the light into the darkness to set others free to walk in the light. When we live in the truth, we understand that the pain of exposure to the light is a good pain designed by God to burn away pits of darkness and turn us into children of light. "For you were once darkness, but now you are light in the Lord. Live as children of light (for the fruit of the light consists in all goodness, righteousness and truth)."[19]

God's judgment is against those who "suppress the truth"[20] and create false narratives, which we described in chapter 4. False narratives are not just "spin" or even "brand protection," though they may be that, too. They are *darkness*. They are the opposite of light.

James, in his epistle, identifies two nasty features of being human and offers some wise counsel: "If you are bitterly jealous and there is selfish ambition in your heart, don't cover up the truth with boasting and lying."[21] I (Scot) want to clarify the translation of the word *jealous*, which is taken from the Greek term *zelos*. James is pointing to the desire to overpower others. He's talking about powerful people using their power to overcome the weak. What motivates false narratives is a zealous ambition to protect a brand, defend a reputation, or preserve the glory of an ambitious leader, a zealous church, and its board of leaders.

Mike Breaux, a former teaching pastor at Willow Creek, shared the devastating effects of truth suppression to the soul during a return visit to the church in January 2019.

That's how it starts—it's just a little exaggeration; just a little embellishment; just a little political spin; and before you know it, authenticity takes a leave of absence in our [lives], and we're no longer real.

And why do we do that, anyway? . . . Sometimes we hide the truth to project an image, sometimes we do it to protect a brand. Sometimes we do it to cover our tracks. We do it to stay in power. . . .

I watched some really good, kind, humble, noble people thrown under the bus, and their families deeply affected. . . . Withholding the truth destroys families— families like yours, families like mine, families like this one. And transparency and truth sets you free. . . .

And while it's absolutely true that the truth will set you free, it's also true it can make you miserable for a while. . . . But here's what I know: Truth always leads to growth and freedom on the other side.[22]

WHEN CHURCHES RESIST TRUTH TELLING

What happens when a church refuses to listen, when the leaders deny, deny, deny and continue to propagate a false narrative? What happens when the church decides to circle the wagons to preserve their brand, their reputation, and their narrative? What happens when all channels for revealing the truth have been exhausted? Sometimes the truth tellers must go public because the church's false narratives are suppressing the truth.

As difficult as it might be to revisit the pain of abuse, people who have been wounded *want* their stories to be told. They want their pain to be acknowledged and the truth to be known. People who have been abused *need* for the truth to be told so they can begin the process of healing. But just as those who have been abused want the truth revealed, the perpetrators want the story covered up and silenced.

For reasons we've already explored, and often under the guise of "being biblical," church leaders commonly ask victims and survivors and their supporters not to go public, but to maintain the "dignity" of silence. But if darkness needs the light in order to root out evil, sometimes the most biblical thing we can do is to expose evil to the light of truth by going public. Certainly, whenever possible one should go to the offender one-on-one before involving others. But that is never the case when there has been sexual abuse or abuse of power. Asking a victim to confront the abuser in that way is abuse in itself.

Keri Ladouceur told me (Laura) that when she complained that Bill Hybels's behavior toward her was inappropriate, two Willow Creek leaders encouraged her to meet one-on-one with Hybels (Matthew 18 again) to discuss her concerns with him. Keri was told her feedback would be "a gift to Bill" and that he needed to hear feedback about situations "that could have been misinterpreted." It felt to Keri that assumptions were being made and conclusions had already been drawn. Still, she was willing to meet with Hybels for the sake of the truth. But she was adamant that she didn't want to meet with him *alone*. Several times, Keri said, she asked for and was refused permission to have a neutral third party in attendance. Feeling it would be unwise to meet with Hybels one-on-one, she prudently decided not to.[23]

If a church and its leadership continue to not listen, if they continue to control the narrative with less-than-truthful or blatantly false narratives, then it is biblical—and best—to go public.

Let's dig a bit deeper on this question. The Bible's language for "going public" is *prophetic action*. And it's all over the Bible. Throughout the Old Testament, when leaders were suppressing the truth and living out a false narrative, the prophets sometimes acted out God's message to get people's attention. Jeremiah broke a pot in public to demonstrate what God was about to do.[24] On another occasion, he took a clean linen belt and buried it in a hill. Later, he recovered it as a useless garment—all to act out God's judgment on the people for their sins.[255]

The prophets were not called to the negotiating table. They were not called to conference rooms or offices or the local coffee shop to converse and reconcile. They were called to the platform of public proclamation. When leaders in the church suppress the truth, it is profoundly biblical to go public. Anything less than bringing the truth to light would be profoundly *un*biblical.

Prophetic action and proclamation have been the agents of truth telling, repentance, and restoration throughout the history of the Bible and the church. But let's be clear: Prophetic action should never be the *first* thing someone does. In the case of Willow Creek, the survivors and their advocates waited for four years before they went public. When interpersonal and behind-closed-doors options were exhausted, prophetic public action became biblically warranted. It was shocking for us to discover that, for four years, the women at Willow Creek had privately begged for the truth to be told, but leadership had pleaded with them not to go public and publicly chided those who did. It was even more disturbing to hear from at least a dozen people that the church was offering large sums of money in exchange for silence and nondisclosure agreements.

If the *Chicago Tribune* hadn't published the story by Manya Brachear Pashman and Jeff Coen, it is likely the women would still be pleading and Willow Creek would still be delaying. But this is not just about one church. Time and time again, survivors who have chosen goodness and truth, who told their stories privately and followed the church's processes, have been silenced. The truth was suppressed and the perpetrators remained in their powerful positions. Churches that have used a maintain-the-silence strategy have forced bloggers, journalists, and authors into a public reckoning. When powerful perpetrators and church leaders refuse to do what's right, it is time for prophetic, biblical action. It is time to go public.

MODELING YOM KIPPUR

Although human history began with hiding and an attempted cover-up, the Bible is not complicit in concealing sin. Anyone who has ever read Scripture knows that people in the Bible are shown for who they are—warts and all. Abraham lied about his wife—*twice*—to save his own skin. Jacob deceived his father to steal his brother's birthright. Joseph's brothers sold him into slavery and then faked his death to fool their father. Moses killed an Egyptian and fled into the desert, where he lived in exile for forty years. David was an adulterer who schemed to kill a woman's husband. Then there was Solomon, with his seven hundred wives and three hundred concubines. It would take too many pages to describe him. In the New Testament, James and John jockeyed for power and position among the disciples and wanted to call down lightning from heaven to destroy a village that shunned Jesus. Peter at one point denied he even knew Jesus and years later got into an ugly spat with Paul.

Reading the Bible is not like reading fairy tales that all have happy endings. God is willing to tell the truth about our human failings. And he wants us to tell the truth, as well. He also had a story of his own to tell—about atonement, forgiveness, and reconciliation. It is the story of Yom Kippur, and it contains an important lesson for us today.

Every year, since time immemorial, Israel has celebrated Yom

Kippur, the Day of Atonement, a day on which the nation tells the truth about itself, and Israel's *tov* God forgives the people with an utterly gracious forgiveness.

Along with the sacrifice that purified the Temple as a place fit for God's dwelling, and along with the obvious need for Israel—as a people and as individuals—to be purified of sin, three themes are central to Yom Kippur:

1. Everyone gathers together.
2. Everyone denies themselves physical pleasures (fasting from food and water, no bathing or anointing of the body, and no sexual relations).
3. No one works.

Yom Kippur, then, is a congregational act of focused self-denial to concentrate the people's minds on God, on their sins of the past year, and on the grace of God's forgiveness and reconciliation. Here's what the Bible says about this holiday:

Then the LORD said to Moses, "Be careful to celebrate the Day of Atonement on the tenth day of that same month—nine days after the Festival of Trumpets. You must observe it as an official day for holy assembly, a day to deny yourselves and present special gifts to the LORD. Do no work during that entire day because it is the Day of Atonement, when offerings of purification are made for you, making you right with the LORD your God. All who do not deny themselves that day will be cut off from God's people. And I will destroy anyone among you who does any work on that day. You must not do any work at all! This is a permanent law for you, and it must be observed from generation to generation wherever you live. This will be a Sabbath day of complete rest for you, and on that day you must deny yourselves. This day of rest will begin at sundown on the ninth day of the month and extend until sundown on the tenth day."[26]

A commitment to confession, repentance, sacrifice, purification, and forgiveness were at the heart of Jewish culture. Along with the ordinary, run-of-the-mill sacrifices connected to sins, Israel set aside an entire calendar event to remember and confess their sin and to get right with their *tov* God.

In our day, we are called to confess our sin to God and to one another.[27] Confession means to admit, to name, to describe, and to own up to what we have done. We are reconciled with God through our confessions. To attempt to "move on" past our sin without truth-telling confession is to cheapen God's grace.

The expression "cheap grace" comes from Dietrich Bonhoeffer's famous book *The Cost of Discipleship*. Here are some of his penetrating words:

> Cheap grace means grace as bargain-basement goods, cut-rate forgiveness, cut-rate comfort, cut-rate sacrament; grace as the church's inexhaustible pantry, from which it is doled out by careless hands without hesitation or limit. It is grace without a price, without costs. . . .
>
> The church that teaches this doctrine of grace thereby confers such grace upon itself. The world finds in this church a cheap cover-up for its sins, for which it shows no remorse and from which it has even less desire to be set free. . . .
>
> Cheap grace means justification of sin but not of the sinner. . . .

Cheap grace is preaching forgiveness without repentance; it is baptism without the discipline of community; it is the Lord's Supper without confession of sin; it is absolution without personal confession. Cheap grace is grace without discipleship, grace without the cross, grace without the living, incarnate Jesus Christ.[28]

Just as grace is not cheap but was purchased for us by the shed blood of Jesus Christ, telling the truth comes at a cost, as well.

When Pat Baranowski's story of abuse at the hands of Bill Hybels was published in the *New York Times*, Steve Carter, Willow Creek's leading teaching pastor, was physically sickened by what he read and by what he now recognized as an inappropriately toxic response from the church's leaders. "After many frank conversations with our elders," he said, "it became clear that there is a fundamental difference in judgment between what I believe is necessary for Willow Creek to move in a positive direction, and what they think is best."[29]

Steve pleaded with Willow Creek's leaders for truth and transparency, but when his appeals went unheaded, he resigned his position as teaching pastor, saying, "It would be misleading of me to stand on that stage as if presenting a unified front."[30]

The way we see it, Steve's decision to abruptly leave Willow Creek was prophetic. His public act of immediately resigning spoke louder than words ever could. His decision was courageous, it was honest, and it *put people first*, ahead of his own interests. In short, it was a decision for *tov*.

Similar stories could be told about some of the elders at Harvest Bible Chapel who resigned from the board after repeated attempts to hold James MacDonald accountable fell on deaf ears with the rest of the elders. Some of those men even suffered the humiliation of being publicly excommunicated from fellowship at Harvest and having their decision to go public called "satanic to the core."[31]

Truth telling is difficult, but Yom Kippur is all about telling the truth, for it is only through honest confession that the darkness of sin can be brought to light and exposed to the atoning blood of Christ.

SKIPPING YOM KIPPUR

On July 19, 2019, some sixteen months after the *Chicago Tribune* printed its revelations about Bill Hybels, Willow Creek's new elder board emailed a letter to the congregation that finally seemed to recognize the need for what we are calling a Yom Kippur moment—a time of confession, lament, repentance, forgiveness, and reconciliation.[32] The elders recognized Hybels's "denials and failure to acknowledge sinful, intimidating, and overly controlling behavior."[33] And they acknowledged the harm suffered by many through "broken relationships, trust, and sense of community."[34] These are biblically sound confessions. The letter included an apology to the women and their supporters, which was also posted on the church's website:

> To the women and their advocates: In the days and months following the March 2018 *Chicago Tribune* article, the church's response led to verbal and written attacks. We have heard about the impact this has had on you, your families, and your professional standing within the Christian community. We learned that the narrative persists in identifying you as liars and colluders despite the apology released by the lead pastors in June 2018 and the former Elders in August 2018. In early 2019,

the IAG report found your allegations to be credible, and
we unequivocally support their findings. We believe your
allegations about Bill. We ask anyone who participated in
verbal and written attacks to prayerfully examine their
actions, apologize for wrongdoing, and seek to mend the
relationship.[35]

When the letter concluded by inviting "all past and present
Willow family to join the Elders for a worship and reflection
service," it seemed they might be setting into place the pieces
for a corporate, Yom Kippur–like time of confession and grieving. Sadly, what transpired at the meeting was another example
of institutional betrayal that served only to retraumatize the
wounded.[36] Though the elders acknowledged that the church
had been "marred by power abuse, sexual sin, and idolatry,"[37]
they didn't address the underlying culture that had allowed Bill
Hybels's sinful habits to go unchecked. Though they made reference to "unaddressed sin going on and men and women being
hurt,"[38] they didn't speak to the power dynamics that had covered
up the sin or apologize for publicly and intentionally accusing
the women and their supporters of collusion and lying. And they
didn't address the cultural dynamics at Willow Creek that led so
many in the congregation to side with Bill Hybels against the
women. Instead, they attempted to pivot to a message of reconciliation and their vision for the future—in short, let's make up
and move on. But reconciliation isn't possible without confession
and repentance. When the apostle Paul told the Corinthians that
God "reconciled us to himself through Christ,"[39] the *cost* of that
reconciliation was clearly understood. But when the new Willow
Creek elder board declared that the congregational email would
be their "last public statement intended to directly address the

events of 2018," they effectively skipped Yom Kippur in favor of cheap grace.

YOM KIPPUR IN CHRISTIAN PRACTICE

Yom Kippur was not a one-and-done event. It was an annual reminder to the people of God to tell the truth about their sins and to seek God's forgiveness.

Likewise, we need a regular Yom Kippur–like season in our churches to ensure that truth telling becomes foundational to our culture. Those congregations that are attentive to the church's traditional calendar may already have the infrastructure in place: the forty-day season of Lent, which comes to its completion in Holy Week. If we combine Lent, which is about grieving our sin through fasting and repentance, with looking forward to the grace of forgiveness expressed on Good Friday and Easter, we will have a solid Christian counterpart to Yom Kippur, complete with introspection, denial, confession, and forgiveness. In churches that do not observe the church calendar, the habit of confession may not be well developed. Or to put it another way, those churches would need to devise a means and a method for confession to become part of the fabric of their culture.

The habit of Lent should enable a church to respond well when a leader fails or when sin occurs within the congregation. Thus, when a church leader fails, the congregation can enter into a Yom Kippur moment to ponder its ways, discern its sins, and seek the grace of God through confession and repentance.

A common refrain among church leaders when sin comes to light and must be dealt with is that they are "going through a season" or "a chapter" in the life of the church. But what exactly are they going through? I (Scot) am convinced that most leaders just want to *get out* of that season, and they don't see it as an opportunity for a redemptive Yom Kippur. But without embracing these Yom Kippur moments—"seasons" of introspection and confession—churches fail to see the depth of their problems, and therefore fail to repent and fail to reconcile with God.

Whether we turn to Yom Kippur or Lent, or to the general Christian practice of confession, we must acknowledge that confession and repentance are required. False narratives must be seen for what they are: *false*. They must be acknowledged and renounced and replaced by a commitment to telling the truth.

Dr. Wade Mullen captured this poetically on Twitter:

Sorrow is feigned,
confession is partial,
forgiveness is exploited,
restitution is an afterthought,
and reconciliation is an illusion,
as long as truth remains unnamed.[40]

As James Baldwin writes in *The Price of the Ticket*, "Whoever cannot tell himself the truth about his past is trapped in it . . . unable to assess either his weaknesses or his strengths, and how frequently indeed he mistakes the one for the other."[41] He urges us to tell the truth, to tell that history, even if the "price of this is a long look backward" with a necessary "unflinching assessment of the record."[42]

Taking inspiration from Baldwin's challenge, and borrowing his words to apply to our purpose, "we have an opportunity" in the church "to create, finally, what we must have had in mind when we first began."[43] But if we want to seize that opportunity in churches where dark forces have led to sinful behavior, abuse, cover-ups, false narratives, and blatant public lies, it can be accomplished only by taking that long look backward and making an unflinching assessment of the record. It will require a Yom Kippur moment, like the one initiated by Robert Cunningham at Tates Creek Presbyterian Church (see chapter 3). If pastors and elders and congregations want to lead their churches to healing, they must choose not to skip God's design of confession, repentance, forgiveness, and reconciliation. They must face the past squarely, with the courage of God's gracious love.

In the spirit of naming the truth, we encourage churches to develop a litany of confession through which pastors, leaders, and the congregation can admit to God and to one another their complicity, their sinfulness, and their failing of *all* who have been abused or exploited in the church. Here we offer an example of a liturgy that a church like Willow Creek—the example we're most familiar with—could use after determining the truth of a sinful situation.

> *Lord, in your mercy, hear our prayer.*
> There is evidence that Bill Hybels's accusers told the truth about him, that he abused them with his behavior and his words.
> We believe Bill was wrong.
> We believe we were wrong for supporting a culture that allowed abusive behavior to occur and continue.
> We lament the way his accusers were treated.
> We apologize, seek their forgiveness, and publicly affirm them.
> *Lord, in your mercy, forgive our sins.*
>
> *Lord, in your mercy, hear our prayer.*
> We believe Pat Baranowski told the truth about Bill Hybels.

We lament for the way Pat was treated, and we lament
for the years of depression, poverty, and isolation that
followed.

We apologize to Pat and ask her forgiveness.

We publicly acknowledge Pat's courage in coming
forward, and we publicly affirm her.

Lord, in your mercy, forgive our sins.

Lord, in your mercy, hear our prayer.

We believe Vonda Dyer told the truth about Bill Hybels.

We lament for the way Vonda was treated.

We lament for the consequences she suffered by coming
forward.

We repent and we apologize to Vonda and ask her
forgiveness.

We publicly acknowledge Vonda's courage in speaking
out, and we publicly affirm her.

Lord, in your mercy, forgive our sins.

Lord, in your mercy, hear our prayer.

We believe Nancy Beach told the truth about Bill Hybels.

We lament for the consequences she suffered by coming
forward.

We repent and we apologize to Nancy and ask her
forgiveness.

We publicly acknowledge Nancy's courage in speaking
out, and we publicly affirm her.

Lord, in your mercy, forgive our sins.

Lord, in your mercy, hear our prayer.

We believe Julia Williams told the truth about Bill Hybels.

We lament for the way Julia was treated.

We publicly acknowledge her courage in coming forward,
and we publicly affirm her.
Lord, in your mercy, forgive our sins.

Lord, in your mercy, hear our prayer.
We believe Maureen Girkins told the truth about Bill
Hybels.
We lament for the way Maureen was treated.
We publicly acknowledge her courage in coming forward,
and we publicly affirm her.
Lord, in your mercy, forgive our sins.

Lord, in your mercy, hear our prayer.
We believe Keri Ladouceur told the truth about Bill
Hybels.
We lament for the consequences she suffered by coming
forward.
We repent and we apologize to Keri and ask her
forgiveness.
We publicly acknowledge her courage in coming forward,
and we publicly affirm her.
Lord, in your mercy, forgive our sins.

Lord, in your mercy, hear our prayer.
We believe Betty Schmidt told the truth about Bill Hybels.
We lament for the consequences Betty suffered by
speaking out.
We repent and we apologize to Betty and ask her
forgiveness.
We publicly acknowledge her courage in coming forward,
and we publicly affirm her.
Lord, in your mercy, forgive our sins.

Lord, in your mercy, hear our prayer.
We believe Jimmy and Leanne Mellado told the truth
    about Bill Hybels.
We lament for the consequences they suffered by
    speaking out.
We repent and we apologize to Jimmy and Leanne and
    ask their forgiveness.
We publicly acknowledge their courage in bringing these
    events to light, and we publicly affirm them.
Lord, in your mercy, forgive our sins.

Lord, in your mercy, hear our prayer.
We believe Manya Brachear Pashman, Jeff Coen, and Bob
    Smietana are people of journalistic integrity.
We believe Manya and Jeff told the truth about Bill
    Hybels in the *Chicago Tribune.*
We believe Bob told the truth about Bill Hybels in
    Christianity Today.
We lament for the way they were treated.
We repent and we apologize to Manya, Jeff, and Bob and
    ask their forgiveness.
We publicly acknowledge their journalistic skill and
    integrity.
Lord, in your mercy, forgive our sins.

Using the example above, we invite you now to create and pray your own litany for your own church, organization, or situation. If there were multiple perpetrators, multiple incidents, and/or multiple victims, simply repeat the appropriate portions of the litany, changing the names as needed until you have covered every one of the women and men, girls and boys from your church or ministry who need to hear words of confession, repentance, and apology. The litany can be as long as needed to cover all who were affected. You can customize the wording as you see fit, but be sure to include the following essential elements:

1. Affirm the truth teller(s).
2. Name the perpetrator and all specific wrongdoing.
3. Confess all complicity (whether intentional or by neglect) of other leaders and the congregation.
4. Publicly acknowledge the harm done to the victim(s), express sorrow, lament, confession, and repentance, and ask for forgiveness.
5. Publicly acknowledge the desire/intention to change.

Telling the truth is at the heart of the Circle of *Tov*, but truth telling is not instinctive in toxic cultures where false narratives proliferate. It must be developed. In a church called *tov*, truth telling becomes a way of life, a way of constant exposure to our *tov* God who reveals himself in Jesus Christ. In God's grace, the Holy Spirit opens us to the truth. As we embrace the truth, the Spirit turns us into a committed band of truth tellers who seek justice, which is the next attribute we'll examine in the Circle of *Tov*.

10

TOV CHURCHES NURTURE JUSTICE

IN A *TOV* CHURCH CULTURE, justice—doing the right thing—is a leading theme. In a toxic church culture, loyalty to the leader or brand often takes precedence. At times, the difference between justice and loyalty is subtle, but when they are at odds with one another, those differences become massive. Sadly, in many churches today, Christians are asked to choose between loyalty and justice.

A HERO OF RESISTANCE

Rachael Denhollander, a former gymnast, received international attention when she became the first woman to publicly accuse the well-known and respected team physician for USA Gymnastics, Larry Nassar, of sexual assault. Nassar was a prominent osteopath with offices at Michigan State University—where he treated, and repeatedly abused, Rachael and hundreds of other young female athletes who were his patients. Nassar is now imprisoned for life as a result of Rachael's, and others', committed advocacy efforts to bring him to justice as a serial sexual abuser of children and young women.[1] Rachael said that she came forward into the public light "because it was right."[2]

Who among us can forget Rachael's televised testimony and the moment when she faced Nassar in the courtroom and made a soul-wrenching statement about forgiveness for her abuser?

> You spoke of praying for forgiveness. But Larry, if you have read the Bible you carry, you know forgiveness does not come from doing good things, as if good deeds can erase what you have done. It comes from repentance, which requires facing and acknowledging the truth about what you have done in all of its utter depravity and horror without mitigation, without excuse, without acting as if good deeds can erase what you have seen in this courtroom today. . . .
>
> The Bible . . . carries a final judgment where all of God's wrath and eternal terror is poured out on men like you. Should you ever reach the point of truly facing what you have done, the guilt will be crushing. And that is what makes the gospel of Christ so sweet. Because it extends grace and hope and mercy where none should be found. And it will be there for you.
>
> I pray you experience the soul crushing weight of guilt so you may someday experience true repentance and true forgiveness from God, which you need far more than forgiveness from me—though I extend that to you as well.[3]

Our purpose here is not to focus on Rachael's success in bringing Larry Nassar to justice, as important as that was, but rather to highlight her tireless efforts to expose evidence of sexual abuse within the Sovereign Grace Churches (SGC) network.[4] What Rachael discovered was a fierce and unbending loyalty to the SGC institution rather than a willingness to pursue justice for abused children, men, and women. Sadly, she received more support for bringing Larry Nassar to justice than she did for exposing the sin of SGC's various pastors and leaders.

In Rachael's courtroom testimony during the Nassar trial, she said, "My advocacy for sexual assault victims, something I cherished, cost me my church and our closest friends three weeks before I filed my police report. I was left alone and isolated."[5] She is referring to her decision to leave Immanuel Baptist Church in Louisville, Kentucky, after Sovereign Grace Church leader C. J. Mahaney was invited to preach at the church.[6]

Prior to this invitation, Rachael had expressed concerns to church elders about allowing Mahaney to preach because of the allegations against him and the leaders in his church of covering up sexual abuse within their network of churches. She was then labeled "divisive" by church leaders and was told by an Immanuel Baptist pastor, "You cannot discuss SGC in any context where another member might hear that your position differs from the leadership's."[7] That is a classic example of placing loyalty before truth.

In most instances, loyalty is a virtue, but not when it obstructs justice and prevents people from doing what is right before God. Within the toxic culture of the Sovereign Grace network, people who spoke up were often depicted as disloyal. Women at SGC said they were discouraged from divorcing abusive husbands, and pastors who were accused of abuse remained in church leadership.[8] When abuse survivors bravely disclosed their stories to pastors and leaders, they were told to resolve their "differences" according to

Matthew 18 and 1 Corinthians 6, and that the abuse should not be reported to civil authorities. Going to the authorities would be disloyal and "unbiblical." What dominated the culture? Loyalty to the pastors, to the elders, and to the church and its network of churches. (In 2019, SGC issued a statement saying, "We categorically deny the accusations of covering up abuse and protecting abusers.")[9]

In a 2018 interview with *Christianity Today*, Rachael Denhollander said she believes "church is one of the least safe places to acknowledge abuse," and "church is one of the worst places to go for help."[10] In her memoir, Rachael reveals being abused as a child by a college student at her church. Counselors had warned church leaders about this college student, recognizing signs of grooming and physical overfamiliarity. But the church leaders discounted concerns about the student because the counselors "used materials by psychologists and licensed therapists" that were "'outside Scripture,' so they couldn't be trusted."[11] She said other occurrences of abuse had been reported at her childhood church, only to be kept secret in an effort to preserve the church's reputation. Again, loyalty prevailed over justice.

When, as an adult, Rachael raised concerns about how abuse allegations were handled at SGC, church leaders used Rachael's history as a survivor of abuse in an effort to discredit her. An Immanuel Baptist pastor told her she was "projecting her own experiences."[12]

What Rachael and her husband, Jacob, encountered was loyalty to the institution at the cost of justice for the sexually abused. Rachael recounts in her memoir that Jacob was asked to step down from a volunteer position at the church, and the church shut down their care group—all because she had questioned the elder board.[13]

> The reason I lost my church was not specifically because
> I spoke up. It was because we were advocating for other

victims of sexual assault within the evangelical community,
crimes which had been perpetrated by people in the
church and whose abuse had been enabled, very clearly,
by prominent leaders in the evangelical community. That
is not a message that evangelical leaders want to hear,
because it would cost to speak out about the community.
It would cost to take a stand against these very prominent
leaders, despite the fact that the situation we were dealing
with is widely recognized as one of the worst, if not *the*
worst, instances of evangelical cover-up of sexual abuse.
Because I had taken that position, and because we were not
in agreement with our church's support of this organization
and these leaders, it cost us dearly.[14]

In the end, prominent SGC leaders defended one another,
C. J. Mahaney was protected, and the pastors at Immanuel Baptist
prayed for the endurance of SGC leaders in the face of the false
assertions against them.[15] Who lost? Truth, justice, and the
wounded.

TOXIC LOYALTY

In our research for this book, we uncovered far too many examples
of loyalty-demanding leaders. Not surprisingly, Bill Hybels's name
came up often. An extensive study of Willow Creek Community
Church by Greg Pritchard, now president of the Forum of
Christian Leaders, revealed a stifling loyalty culture under Hybels's
leadership.

Loyalty became the most prized virtue in the church and
disloyalty one of the greatest vices. One staff member
explained to me that the central unspoken question the

leadership have toward a newcomer is, "Do you really care about the church and this ministry?" When I probed this issue, one central leader admitted, "You're right; the need for loyalty" is "very high."

I discovered during my interviews with staff members a deep fear of being labeled disloyal. . . . The only dissatisfied staff member I found remarked, "They [church leadership] value loyalty more than honesty."[16]

The seeds for loyalty were planted early in the history of Willow Creek and quickly became a deeply rooted feature of its culture. One can assume that everyone in any kind of leadership position was deeply loyal.

Harvest Bible Chapel also placed a premium on loyalty. Here is a disturbing example of how it played out in the culture there:

James [MacDonald]'s favorite game when the leadership team is together at camp or off-site is "The Name Game." He makes everyone put the names of three former HBC employees in a hat, then to go around and draw a name and describe the crappy things the person did until he/she is guessed. Upon reflection, I now realize that this game serves the dual purpose of:

- Getting everyone to openly mock staff people who leave
- Reinforce the pillar of loyalty in Harvest Staff culture; those who leave are bad, and you don't ever want to be one of them.[17]

When Mike Bryant, a pastor formerly in the Harvest church network, fell into disfavor with James MacDonald, his church was

kicked out of the network. After losing half his 300-member congregation and spending tens of thousands of dollars to change
the name of his church, Bryant had this to say about the leadership at Harvest: "They want loyalty above righteousness."[18]
(Righteousness here means "doing the right thing.")

WHY?

Faced with so many examples of church leaders and congregations
who have tolerated sinful behavior by their pastors or other leaders, one can only ask, *Why?*

Why did so many priests and bishops defend the priests
accused of sexually molesting boys and girls? Loyalty to
the Roman Catholic institution?

Why did so many elders—the numbers would boggle your
mind—at Harvest Bible Chapel defend James MacDonald
when they knew of his vulgarity, gambling, and abuse of
power? Loyalty to the man?

Why did leaders at Willow Creek, after they discovered
that Bill Hybels had directed a church employee to
smash Hybels's hard drive to pieces to destroy evidence,
continue to defend him? Loyalty to the name?

Why did Southern Baptist leaders refuse to investigate Mark
Aderholt, and instead nominate and appoint him to
leadership positions, after they knew his sins? Loyalty to
the reputation of the Southern Baptist Convention and its
leaders?

Loyalty to a charismatic leader, the reputation of a ministry, and a church's brand are major obstacles to doing the right thing. Toxic cultures breed misplaced and corrupted loyalty. *Tov* cultures promote doing the right thing even when it requires a seeming *dis*loyalty to the charismatic pastor, the celebrity church, and the inner circles of power. *Tov* cultures are loyal to a higher power— Almighty God—which means a higher standard of honesty, integrity, justice, and righteousness.

WHAT IS JUSTICE?

Because justice is central to a *tov* church culture, we need a good definition. Let's start by looking at some common uses of the word.

"Let's bring these criminals to justice."
"Let's fight for justice."
"Vote for me, vote for justice."
"Your honor, I ask for justice for my client."

When we're talking about criminals, justice often means vengeance or retribution for a wrongful act. In the second instance, justice refers to balancing the scales in society, often having to do with racism or economics. In the third, justice means someone's political platform, as in, "A vote for me is a vote for the kind of justice activism I support." In the fourth, justice refers to impartiality or fairness under the law.

So, what is justice? Equality, fairness, impartiality, goodness, neutrality, a legal decision by one authorized to make decisions? Yes, each, in some way. Notice that each of these terms operates according to a *standard*, so we might say that *the foundation of justice is a standard by which we measure what is just or right*. So whether we're talking about the US Constitution, the letter of the law, or a vague sense of our Western liberalism, we have some standard in mind when we talk about justice.

Christians, of course, define justice according to the Bible. The Christian standard is God's revelation in his Word—both the living Word (Jesus Christ) and the written Word (the Bible). Justice, therefore, can be defined as behavior that measures up to or conforms with what God has revealed to us in Christ and in Scripture. There's no law in our legal system that demands love, but Christ does. There's no law that requires empathy and compassion, but Christ does. There's no law that demands grace, but Christ does. Because of what Christ demands of us, our sense of justice as Christians will be radically different than the world's understanding of justice.

Christian justice is expressed in this potent warning from Jesus: "Unless your righteousness is better than the righteousness of the teachers of religious law and the Pharisees, you will never enter the Kingdom of Heaven!"[19] In other words, Jesus is calling us to behave in ways that measure up to and conform with *his* teachings, not the teachings of the world.

And here's a little secret: The Greek word for righteousness in this verse is *dikaiosune*, which can also be translated "justice." For Jesus, a *righteous* person is someone who follows his teachings. Likewise, a *just* person is someone who follows Christ's teachings. Someone who does not follow his teachings is unrighteous and unjust. A *tov* culture has an instinct for doing the right thing, even in the most challenging moments. Toxic cultures find a way around doing the right thing.

There is an added element in *dikaiosune* that we should note here: The root term *dikaio-* can be translated "justification" in other contexts. This brings in another aspect of doing what is right. In Christian theology, God comes first (God is *tov*, righteous, and full of grace). Only through God's grace, salvation and justification in Christ, and the gift of the Holy Spirit, can we

(1) know God's grace, (2) be just or righteous before God, (3) be *tov*, or (4) do what is right.

Paul captures this in a well-known paragraph in Ephesians: "God saved you by his grace when you believed. And you can't take credit for this; it is a gift from God. Salvation is not a reward for the good things we have done, so none of us can boast about it. For we are God's masterpiece. He has created us anew in Christ Jesus, so we can do the good things he planned for us long ago."[20]

Put into a formula, justice means *to be empowered through the Spirit to do the right thing*. And the "right thing" is *what Jesus teaches*. We have touched on this topic already, so only a brief reminder is needed. God's will is for us to follow the teaching of Jesus, which Jesus himself summarized as *loving God and loving others*—or as Paul teaches, to live in the Spirit of God.[21] We love God by loving others and doing what is right.

THE CIRCLE OF *TOV*
Nurturing Habits of Goodness

TOV

Nurture empathy
Resist a narcissist's culture

Nurture grace
Resist a fear culture

Put people first
Resist institution creep

Tell the truth
Resist false narratives
Know Yom Kippur
Form a truth-telling culture

Nurture justice
Resist the loyalty culture

HOW TO BUILD A JUSTICE CULTURE

When churches get caught up in issues of loyalty, they lose their perspective on doing the right thing. So, what can we teach in our churches to help build a godly standard of justice into the culture?

Know what justice looks like

A justice culture knows what justice *is*: namely, doing what is right at the right time. The "right thing" will always conform to the character and life of Jesus and his mission to establish God's Kingdom on earth. A *tov* culture measures goodness, rightness, and justice by comparing it to Jesus. Years ago, many young people wore bracelets with the inscription WWJD: "What would Jesus do?" It's still a good standard and a good reminder.

Years ago, when I (Scot) was teaching at another seminary in Chicagoland, I had a colleague named Ruth Tucker, who was full of personality and spark. Ruth was the author of a widely read book on missions, and she was working with another colleague of mine, Walt Liefeld, on a book about women in the Bible and church. It, too, became a go-to book.

What wasn't widely known at the time was that Ruth was in a horrifically abusive marriage, which she hid by wearing long sleeves and turtleneck sweaters. When I read Ruth's book titled *Black and White Bible, Black and Blue Wife*, I was grieved (as were Laura and my wife, Kris) to learn not only about Ruth's abusive marriage, but about the shame that had compelled her into silence. But as I read the book, I was proud to know that when Ken Meyer, then-president of the seminary, found out what Ruth was enduring, he did the right thing: he listened, he grieved, and he promised and provided protection.

Ruth eventually disentangled herself from that abusive marriage and went on to have a flourishing career as a teacher and author, still with plenty of personality and spark. Her story is worth reading.

Like the Good Samaritan in Jesus' famous parable, Ken Meyer did the right thing. He saw an injustice, he intervened appropriately, and he offered compassionate care where it was needed. The Good Samaritan saw what was right even when the religious establishment leaders were more concerned with protecting their reputations and external sanctity—following the path of loyalty to a set of rules and regulations, one might say. Perhaps most important, Ken *believed* Ruth. This is something I (Laura) hear a lot from the abused: They want to be believed, first and foremost, and then protected.

Recognize injustice

A justice culture develops deep moral perceptions to recognize injustice. Sometimes these sensibilities emerge from our own experience. During the early days of the church, the Jewish believers went through tough times. James, the brother of Jesus, knew what it was like (almost certainly) to grow up without a father (as most scholars believe Joseph's absence in the Gospels indicates he had died). So James could say, "Religion that God our Father accepts as pure and faultless is this: to look after orphans and widows in their distress and to keep oneself from being polluted by the world."[22] By the way, children in first-century Israel were reckoned to be orphans if they had lost one parent; so when James refers to "orphans and widows," he's no doubt talking about his own family's experience with charity and justice.

Knowing a bit about James's family history helps us to appreciate the strong words he has for the rich who deprive workers of their wages, and it made him sensitive to the poor Jewish believers who were being degraded in public assemblies. James chapter 2 could be written today about the failure of our wealthy, celebrity-struck churches to do the right thing.

My dear brothers and sisters, how can you claim to have
faith in our glorious Lord Jesus Christ if you favor some
people over others?

For example, suppose someone comes into your
meeting dressed in fancy clothes and expensive jewelry,
and another comes in who is poor and dressed in dirty
clothes. If you give special attention and a good seat to
the rich person, but you say to the poor one, "You can
stand over there, or else sit on the floor"—well, doesn't
this discrimination show that your judgments are guided
by evil motives?

Listen to me, dear brothers and sisters. Hasn't God
chosen the poor in this world to be rich in faith? Aren't
they the ones who will inherit the Kingdom he promised
to those who love him? But you dishonor the poor! Isn't it
the rich who oppress you and drag you into court? Aren't
they the ones who slander Jesus Christ, whose noble
name you bear?

Yes indeed, it is good when you obey the royal law as
found in the Scriptures: "Love your neighbor as yourself."
But if you favor some people over others, you are
committing a sin. You are guilty of breaking the law.[23]

Here we have a graphic description of Christians who believe
Jesus is Messiah and Lord yet are denigrating the poor by asking them to sit on the floor while the rich are offered the cushy
seats. And because James knows what justice is, he recognizes
injustice.

But he doesn't stop there; he courageously enters the fray,
calling out the abusers and those who would enable them. It was
the rich who were persecuting the believers; it was the rich who
exploited the poor; and it was the rich who degraded the name

of Jesus. And James says to the church, "You want to favor them in your assemblies? You've got it backwards. Do the right thing!"

You can be certain it cost him to say and do the right thing, because the rich had all the power. But James saw the injustice and did the right thing for the poor. The parallels to our day and age are obvious.

Recognize the fallout, and press on

Those who would form a goodness culture of justice will do the right thing regardless of the fallout. Sometimes this means admitting fault and confessing sin, and sometimes it means coming under attack and taking hits. Think of Robert Cunningham, who told the truth about what had happened at Tates Creek Presbyterian Church. Think of Rachael Denhollander and the fallout she experienced for confronting church abuse. Think of all the people at Willow Creek Community Church and Harvest Bible Chapel who suffered reproach, resistance, and even character assassination as they persisted in calling out the sins of their leaders. Doing the right thing requires courage. A church called *tov* will be filled with courageous people who do the right thing.

Tell stories about doing the right thing

We all need to tell stories of when justice prevails. And we need to tell the *full* story, not just the victory parts. (Remember the Bible's warts-and-all approach.) For example, do you know the story of Martin Niemöller?

Niemöller was a contemporary and an associate of the well-known Dietrich Bonhoeffer in Hitler's Germany. Drawn into pastoring after a proud military career as a U-boat officer in World War I, he became an ardent German nationalist and was bitter about the treatment of Germans under the Versailles Treaty. As a pastor, he supported the National Socialists, though he never officially joined the Nazi Party. But he twice voted for Hitler.

When the crackdown began, he did not defend the Jews as Jews initially, but only if they were Jewish Christians, and only slowly did he recognize his own anti-Semitism. But he defied Hitler's crossing of the line between church and state, and he protested the "German Christian" movement with its blasphemous blending of church and state. He was arrested by the Nazis in 1937 for opposing Hitler's imposition on the church. After being held for eight months for trial, he was given a seven-month sentence, and thus should have been released. Instead, Hitler personally had him sent to the Sachsenhausen concentration camp, and later to Dachau, where he remained until 1945. In all, he was imprisoned for the better part of a decade.[24]

After the war, he exaggerated the dimensions of his and the church's opposition to Hitler, yet he was the first to acknowledge publicly from the German pastoral community, in terms and tones of confession, that the German people bore guilt and that the pastors had not spoken against Hitler often enough or clearly enough. Nevertheless, he learned from his experience, repented, and confessed. He embraced his own Yom Kippur moments and became known for doing the right thing.

Martin Niemöller's life is a paradigm of social, political, and moral transformation. Any reading of his life will help pastors (especially) and others become more patient with themselves and others, and perhaps encourage them to tell their own stories honestly—stories of growth, of changing course, and of doing the right thing.

Niemöller might be best known for a series of couplets that reflect a dawning self-awareness. He used various versions of these lines in his speeches, and other variations have been attributed to him over the years.

When the Nazis came for the Communists, I did not
speak out.
I was not a Communist.
When they came for the Trade Unionists, I did not speak
out.
I was not a Trade Unionist.
When they came for the Jews, I did not speak out.
I was not a Jew.
When they came for me, there was no one left to speak
out.[25]

When most Christians today think of Germany and the church
during World War II, they think of Dietrich Bonhoeffer. But for a
decade or more after the war, Martin Niemöller, not Bonhoeffer,
was the story.[26] He taught people to know justice so they could
recognize injustice and do the right thing.

11

TOV CHURCHES NURTURE SERVICE

LAURA AND I, ALONG WITH OUR SPOUSES, Mark and Kris, were in Oxford, England, ready to venture for two days into the quaint of all quaints, a region called the Cotswolds. The English countryside there is marked by yellow stone buildings, as well as beautiful grassy and farmed fields, spotted with cattle and sheep and separated by aged hand-stacked stone walls.

Our venturing required leasing a car, and the one we got was very similar to our own car at home. It seated four comfortably, had air conditioning, a radio and CD player, power steering, power windows, and a mapping device with a screen for the driver and everyone else to watch (and tell the driver what to do). In short, everything we needed. There was only one problem—well, two. The steering wheel was on the passenger side, and we had to drive on the wrong side of the road. That's an American bias, to be sure, but perhaps you'll forgive me my bias because everything was *completely the same and completely different* at the same time. When I arrived at a corner, I had to overcome decades-old habits and instincts and look to the other side of the road. When I turned, when I backed up, when I parked—everything was so much the same and yet so different that driving for only a few hours exhausted everyone in the car.

A pastor who makes himself the center of attention and a pastor who serves the congregation have all the same standard equipment. They both preach and teach and form committees and share vision and administer missions and motivate and encourage and all the things we've come to expect from our pastors. And yet they couldn't be more different.

In a toxic culture, the celebrity pastor finds a way to make it all about garnering praise for himself—his vision, his ministry, his success, his glory. He may not always state it in such bald-faced terms, but if you scratch beneath the surface, you'll find that people don't matter, the institution matters; power and fear dominate the culture; the only narratives told are those that prop up the pastor's vision and success; and loyalty is the supreme virtue.

For the servant pastor, everything is different. A culture of service turns everyone toward one another instead of toward themselves. People are first, grace matters, empathy is a first response, truth is told, and doing what is right shapes the mission of the church.

To be clear, the size of the church does not matter. What matters is the size of the pastor's ego.

Think of it this way: In a *tov* church, leaders maximize their giftedness when they *empower others* to maximize their own giftedness. As Paul says in Ephesians 4: "Christ himself gave the apostles, the prophets, the evangelists, the pastors and teachers, to equip his people for works of service, so that the body of Christ may be built up until we all reach unity in the faith and in the knowledge of the Son of God and become mature, attaining to the whole measure of the fullness of Christ."[1] Likewise, *tov* leaders will empower and encourage everyone in the body of Christ to "motivate one another to acts of love and good works."[2]

THE CIRCLE OF *TOV*
Nurturing Habits of Goodness

Nurture empathy
Resist a narcissist's culture

Nurture service
Resist the celebrity culture

TOV

Nurture grace
Resist a fear culture

Nurture justice
Resist the loyalty culture

Put people first
Resist institution creep

Tell the truth
Resist false narratives
Know Yom Kippur
Form a truth-telling culture

THE BALANCING ACT OF SERVICE

Four verses from the Gospel of Mark tell us what we need to hear. When Jesus realized that his closest followers were in a contest of honor and fame, jockeying for the seats closest to Jesus in the Kingdom of God, he said this about his own embodied life:

> You know that the rulers in this world lord it over their people, and officials flaunt their authority over those

under them. But among you it will be different. Whoever wants to be a leader among you must be your servant, and whoever wants to be first among you must be the slave of everyone else. For even the Son of Man came not to be served but to serve others and to give his life as a ransom for many.[3]

Jesus was completely against the celebrity culture that was quickly forming among a few of his closest followers. James and John in particular were beginning to imagine themselves as MVPs of the apostolic band. But Jesus reset the bar for them.

The temptation here is obvious: Self-concern and self-care must be balanced by an others-orientation or we will become self-intoxicated celebrities in our own minds. But even an attitude of service has its temptationsn others-orientation must be balanced with self-care or we will lose ourselves entirely.

There may already be a published spectrum or scale some-where that maps our two extremes—those who live for themselves and those who live for others—but for the purpose of our discussion, we'll use this simple diagram to illustrate how pastors and congregations, as a group and as individuals, must balance self-care and serving others in creating a church called *tov*.

PASTORS

People-pleaser ——————————————————— Celebrity

Serving others ——————————————————— Serving self

CHURCHES
Tov

Some pastors and congregations tend to the left and others tend right; some toward serving others and some toward serv-ing themselves; some toward pleasing others and some toward narcissism and celebrity. Likewise, some celebrity churches think their church alone is truly the best and (perhaps) the only faithful church in the entire world.

On the other hand, some churches are so given to serving others that they burn themselves out with people pleasing. They don't sit around pondering their own greatness, but they tend to exhaust themselves to the point of giving up (or hoping someone else takes on the challenges of serving others).

In a *tov* church, there is a beautiful balance between individual people and the church as a whole. People are served and people serve others. Pastors serve and are served. Churches serve and are served. It's a balancing act, an act filled with temptations—not least for those with a strong (and noble) orientation toward serving others.

TEMPTATIONS FOR SERVICE-ORIENTED CHURCHES

The desire to create a service-oriented culture in the church comes with a big pitfall or potential trap: namely, serving to be *seen* or *celebrated*.

The first way this can happen is by taking service to the heroic extreme: giving up all one's money, selling one's home and clothes, and venturing off into the sacrificial life of serving the poorest of the poorest of the poor—with a corresponding press release. After all, didn't Jesus tell the rich young ruler to sell his possessions and give to the poor?[4] When the greatest Christian act is serving others, some people will pursue greatness by serving others. But pursuing *greatness* is not *tov*.

The second way is perhaps more common: drawing attention to how sacrificial our service is. Before long, we're telling self-saturated stories about our sacrifices (either as individuals or as a church), to great, self-congratulatory applause. This approach to servant Christian living is not genuine service; it's an offshoot of celebrity culture. It's the attempt to be heroic by seeming to oppose the heroic norm—all the while patting ourselves on the back. This is not *tov*, and Jesus spoke to it directly:

> When you give to the needy, do not announce it with trumpets, as the hypocrites do in the synagogues and on the streets, to be honored by others. Truly I tell you, they have received their reward in full.[5]

So how do we avoid being drawn into the circle of celebrity, heroism, and self-congratulatory giving? Jesus speaks to that, as well:

> When you give to someone in need, don't let your left hand know what your right hand is doing. Give your gifts in private, and your Father, who sees everything, will reward you.[6]

Churches that form a service culture will attend to these words of Jesus with rigor.

Even if we give with pure intentions and avoid the traps laid out above, we must always be aware of the effects of our service on those we serve. Calvin Miller, a well-known author, pastor, and professor who passed away in 2012, grew up in very serious poverty in the later years of the Great Depression. He and his family were the grateful recipients of charity during those years, but they were also ashamed of their need and wise to the ulterior motive behind it. Observing the irony of it all, he later wrote in his memoir, *Life Is Mostly Edges*:

> I never felt particularly poor until the rich came by in December to leave us a Christmas basket. Each time they

stopped they "tried to win us to the Lord." They meant
well. They were just trying to keep us out of hell until the
next holiday, I think. . . .

Needless to say, we children didn't want to go to those
churches that brought us the baskets. The last place
you want to go worship is the place where the people
need you to be poor so they themselves can feel rich in
the dispensation of their charity. There is something
grandiose about giving a beggar a dime, but there is
nothing grandiose in receiving it. Beggars don't ask for
money so they can think well of themselves, but because
feeling bad about themselves is usually less painful than
starvation.[7]

We can avoid these pitfalls only by creating a genuine service
culture that permeates our lives and the life of the church—a culture in which ordinary actions of service are the norm, in and out
of season, without the need for congratulations or acclaim.

TOV IS ORDINARY

The very concept of *tov*—goodness—is rooted in the ordinary. We
can do good things, certainly, but *goodness* implies an ongoingness
of good things to the point that they become, well, ordinary, or
what poet and essayist Kathleen Norris calls "quotidian."[8] Paula
Gooder suggests that we need a "spirituality of ordinariness."[9]

A life in service to others is not heroic. Rather, it is ordinary people helping ordinary people who happen to be in their
path as they travel through life. It is family serving family. It is
neighbor helping neighbor. It is ordinary pastors serving ordinary folks in the congregation. It is ordinary church folks helping ordinary church folks and nonchurch folks alike. It is doing

very ordinary—yet vital, necessary—things for others. We are too tempted to be heroic and to glorify celebrity.

In some respects, in our contemporary culture, *ordinary* has acquired the connotation of "not good enough." Let's face it: Most people are average, because that's what average means, but being average is seen by many as unacceptable. On a report card, a C feels like an F for a lot of people, and even a B is an insult because everyone wants—and thinks they deserve—an A. That's because everyone thinks they are above average. Think about that for a while, and you'll understand the absurdity of what's happening in our culture. We can't all be special, because *special* would then mean ordinary and we'd need a new word to set ourselves apart. And even *special* has taken on a connotation that seems less than desirable, so maybe we should just be ordinary after all.

Philosopher Dallas Willard spoke of "the obviously well-kept secret of the 'ordinary,'" which is that "it is made to be a receptacle of the divine, a place where the life of God flows."[10] John Ortberg, a student and friend of Willard's, observed that "it was the extent of the ordinariness [in Dallas] that made the *extra*-ordinary so striking. . . . The 'extraordinary' . . . gave him a poise and wonder and playfulness and ease that made people around him feel their *extra*-ordinariness a little more strongly."[11] That's ordinary, that's okay, and that's what it means to serve others.

Dwight Moody is a good example of a celebrated pastor who did the ordinary.

Moody hosted a large contingent of European pastors at one of his Northfield, Massachusetts, Bible conferences. The pastors were housed in a dormitory and, according to European custom, they all placed their shoes outside their rooms overnight anticipating that a servant boy would collect them, clean them, and shine them before morning. Except this was Massachusetts and not England. No servant boys would appear.

But Moody noticed the shoes. He refused to embarrass the pastors for their cultural ignorance or rebuke them for their presumption. Instead, he quietly gathered the shoes, took them to his room, and shined them himself. The next morning, Moody's pastor friends dutifully collected their shined shoes none the wiser for the humble service Moody had rendered on their behalf.

But there's more to the story. Servanthood is contagious.

It turns out one of the pastors witnessed what Moody did in secret. The astonished pastor told a few of his friends. And from that night on a conspiracy of servanthood took charge of the shoe-shining detail. Pastors privately took turns shining their colleagues' shoes throughout the remainder of the conference.[12]

Now that's *tov*, wouldn't you agree?

RESISTING A CELEBRITY CULTURE

We'll get back to the discussion about forming a service culture later in the chapter, but for now we want to drill down a little more on the celebrity culture we need to resist. There are many temptations for pastors and churches to slide to the right on the scale on page 178. The further we move along that side of the scale, the more likely we are to fall prey to the "celebrity syndrome" that undergirds a celebrity culture. So we must learn how to keep the celebrity culture at bay.

Before we examine ten elements that define "celebrity syndrome," let's repeat one more time that celebrity culture has little to do with the size of the church. Not all big-church or mega-church pastors are celebrities, and some small, rural churches have pastors who *think* they are celebrities. Again, what matters is not the size of the church but the size of the pastor's ego.

Of course, celebrities don't form on their own. Behind every celebrity pastor is an adoring congregation that both loves and supports the celebrity atmosphere. The development of a celebrity culture also doesn't happen overnight. It begins when a pastor has *a driving ambition for fame*, but it can't take root unless the congregation supports that ambition. Unfortunately, many people *want* their pastor to be a spiritual hero or a celebrity at some level. They not only want it, but they often expect it and find themselves believing it about their pastor. Some pastors devour this attention and take it to the next level. Their ambition is to become *known*, and they dream of being "where the lights are shinin' on me," like the line from the Glen Campbell song "Rhinestone Cowboy." Celebrity doesn't happen by chance; it happens intentionally. It must be *pursued* to some degree, by cultivating image, friendships, networks, promoters, and fellow celebrities promoting fellow celebrities.

Despite the image they try to project, it should be noted that too often celebrity pastors *don't actually serve others*, because celebrities tend to see themselves as superior. They are above and beyond the people of their church. Up there on their pedestals, they can't help but tend to think they are *better* than the people of their church. They are treated as such, and they start to believe it. Consider this excerpt from the *Willow Creek Governance Review* report, which examined leadership issues at the church between 2014 and 2018:

> The Senior Pastor was larger than life for many. Most
> board members gave deference to him. This made it

difficult for some elders to challenge him in a meeting. Some of the elders thought they were unwittingly giving him special treatment and tiptoeing around significant issues to prevent conflicts. Some board members struggled with feelings of insecurity when the Senior Pastor was in the room. They felt like they were sitting in board meetings with a celebrity.[13]

Did board members treat Bill Hybels as a celebrity? In our view, no question. Did the ordinary expectations apply to him? Apparently not. The elders gave him special treatment and avoided important issues. He seemed to write his own ticket. Did they treat him as if he were famous? Yes, and he was. Did they have trouble getting along with him? Again, yes. Bill Hybels was a celebrity, but just as important, his elder board *treated him* like a celebrity. The same can be said of other megachurch pastors and even some small-town, small-church pastors who want to be a celebrity and expect to be treated like one. Whatever "service" these celebrity pastors render is often stained with self-enhancement. They don't serve behind the scenes; they serve to be seen and to feed their own egos.

Celebrity pastors live on comparisons, which means they are in *competition* with one another, playing a game called "Who's Got?"

Who's got the best sermons?

Who's got the best outlines?

Who's got the deepest theology?

Who's got the biggest church?

Who's got the biggest opportunity on the biggest conference platforms?

Who's got the biggest Twitter feed?

Who's got the most friends on Facebook?

Who's got the most bestselling books?

Who's got the best employment perks?

Who's got? Who's got? Who's got? It's a treadmill that never stops. I once heard an evangelical leader say he had "the gift of intimidation." What was sad was that it was true and he was proud of it. He liked to think he was winning the "Who's got the most power?" game. But those who are all about "Who's Got?" are playing the wrong game.

Because celebrities see themselves as superior, and they are surrounded by people who treat them as superior, they may easily start to assume they are exempt from ordinary rules and standards. They are confident someone will cover their tracks, explain away their sins, and pave the way for future success. They yell and scream at others, and their bullying behaviors are ignored. When they are not ignored, they are excused. "He's so ambitious," I have heard some enablers say to excuse a celebrity pastor's vices.

Celebrity pastors want *every* Sunday to be a buzz event. They want it to be like crossing the Red Sea, receiving the law at Mount Sinai, building the Temple and seeing the glory of God inhabit the place. They want the Nativity, the Resurrection, the Ascension, and the Second Coming all rolled into one. Celebrity pastors want every Sunday to be glory and smoke and trumpets. They want the music to be the best ever, the vocalists better than last year's, and attendance growing without decline. This is such an American conceit.

Mary DeMuth crafted an insightful piece titled "10 Ways to Spot Spiritual Abuse." She identifies the pastor at the center, yes, but also the culture responsible for creating church celebrities.

As one who has lived overseas, who has viewed the American church from afar, I never would've seen this culture of celebrity had I not ventured elsewhere. We are a commodity and fame-based culture down at our core.

We flock to gurus, project our needs onto them, and latch on [to] those who dine at the cool table. *We contribute to this culture of celebrity by simply needing, demanding and feeding it.*[14]

Celebrity pastors don't arise in service-oriented churches. They need the toxic soil of a celebrity-driven church culture. Amy Simpson, in an article for *Christianity Today*, offers an insightful observation about celebrity syndrome:

Among the factors behind the failures of James MacDonald, Mark Driscoll, and others is a habit of aggressively marginalizing critics and surrounding themselves with people who reinforced their sense of celebrity and cleared obstacles from their paths.[15]

Andy Crouch, executive editor of *Christianity Today* and an astute observer of Christian leaders, maintains that powerful celebrities form a distance between themselves and accountability while creating a persona that others think they know intimately:

That part of the problem—the distance of power and its distorting effects on the powerful—is ancient and will never go away. But it is compounded by something genuinely new: the phenomenon of celebrity. Celebrity combines the old distance of power with what seems like its exact opposite—extraordinary intimacy, or at least a bewitching simulation of intimacy.

It is the power of the one-shot (the face filling the frame), the close mic (the voice dropped to a lover's whisper), the memoir (the disclosures that had never been discussed with the author's pastor, parents, or

sometimes even lover or spouse, before they were
published), the tweet, the selfie, the insta, the snap. All of
it gives us the ability to seem to know someone—without
in fact knowing much about them at all, since in the end
we know only what they, and the systems of power that
grow up around them, choose for us to know.[16]

One of the clearest indicators of this phenomenon is the
up-close-and-personal screens many churches now have that
magnify—uber-magnify is a better term—the image of the pastor
or speaker, who is taught to look at the camera because people
will then feel as if he or she is talking directly to them. It seems so
intimate. (It's not.) Chuck DeGroat, in his book *When Narcissism
Comes to Church*, calls this "fauxnerability," or "a twisted form of
vulnerability."[17]

Accordingly, celebrities help to create a *personality cult* around
themselves. Kate Bowler, in her wonderful book about evangelical
celebrity women, *The Preacher's Wife*, offers an insightful definition of celebrity: "A celebrity is one who actively chases the public
eye, wooing the media and cultivating a network of supporting
agencies and fellow stars that manufactures mass recognition."[18]
That's what every celebrity pastor wants: "mass recognition." The
aim is fame, glory, the main stage.

Bowler observes that a celebrity is both a "person and a product."[19] The words of Simon and Garfunkel from 1964 seem haunt-
ingly prescient of the current age, where churches gloat over their
celebrity pastors to the verge of idolatry: "And the people bowed
and prayed / To the neon god they made."[20]

Let me ask you a few questions: Who was the pastor at
Thessalonica? At Corinth? At Berea? At Ephesus? At Galatia?
There might be a really good reason why we don't know—they
were not celebrities! Even the names we do know—Paul and

Barnabas, Silas, Titus, and Timothy—are not those of pastors who were building their own empires. Instead, they underwent tremendous hardship and testing as they sought to plant churches and spread the good news about Jesus.

The nasty underbelly of celebrity is being *envious* of anyone who might infringe on one's turf and *jealous* for one's own glory. It's a zero-sum game for them. "Either I'm the celebrity or he is, and I want that pedestal." Pride, envy, and jealousy form a distinctive glow around celebrity.

As a pastor grows in visibility and prominence, the aura of celebrity transfers to the congregation, who begin to think of themselves as a *celebrity church*—famous, better than most if not all others, beyond the reach of criticism, and exemplary followers of Jesus. Here's the kicker: When a pastor and a church become celebrities, when visibility, fame, reputation, and branding get the upper hand, the church will no longer be people-first (if it ever was), empathy no longer shapes the culture, grace is subverted, truth is no longer instinctive, and doing what is right can be subverted by works that seek to enhance the church's glory. Such a culture becomes toxic and potentially abusive—especially for those who cross paths or cross wires with the narcissistic pastor at the helm.

Perhaps the number one thing we can do to break the celebrity syndrome is to get off the merry-go-round ourselves. We can start by internalizing the following three statements:

1. There is no such thing as the *most important pastor* in a denomination, in an area, or in America.
2. There is no such thing as the *most important church* in a denomination, in an area, or in America.
3. The terms "celebrity pastor" and "celebrity church" contradict the way of Jesus (and break his heart, by the way).

The desire to be the "most important" is playing the Hollywood game and not the cross-bearing life of Jesus. Your pastor, God bless him or her, is not the most important pastor, but she or he is your pastor and that's all that matters.

JESUS, THE ANTI-CELEBRITY

There is only one who deserves glory, honor, and praise, and that's Jesus, our Lord and King. He refused to play the celebrity game, and he didn't mince words with the celebrity-seeking Pharisees of his day:

> Everything they do is for show. On their arms they wear
> extra wide prayer boxes with Scripture verses inside, and
> they wear robes with extra long tassels. And they love
> to sit at the head table at banquets and in the seats of
> honor in the synagogues. They love to receive respectful
> greetings as they walk in the marketplaces, and to be
> called "Rabbi."[21]

Jesus anticipated the quip about celebrities who are "famous for being famous" and who love being seen. The Pharisees, to make sure they were noticed, made their pious prayer boxes larger to make them more visible. They loved the most important seats and hanging out with other celebrities. And nothing was more precious than being addressed as "Rabbi," which means "my master" or "my lord." It's like being called "Doctor," "Professor," "Father," or "Pastor" today.

Jesus was staunchly against this conspicuous publicity. A good title for him was "servant" or "slave." He was the Servant of all servants. The apostle Paul, too, was against these kinds of titles. Anyone who speaks of others as "the Lord's workers" and "co-workers in God's service," and who refers to himself as "the scum of the earth," is definitely against title-mongering and celebrity-making.[22]

Humble service is the design of Jesus for all his followers because it was the design of his Father for him. He taught service because his own disciples wanted to be celebrities.

Let's take a closer look at Mark 10:32-45, which paints a revealing portrait of the ongoing war between celebrity and humility.

First, let's set the scene:

> They were on their way up to Jerusalem, with Jesus leading the way, and the disciples were astonished, while those who followed were afraid. Again he took the Twelve aside and told them what was going to happen to him. "We are going up to Jerusalem," he said, "and the Son of Man will be delivered over to the chief priests and the teachers of the law. They will condemn him to death and will hand him over to the Gentiles, who will mock him and spit on him, flog him and kill him. Three days later he will rise."[23]

Pretty sobering stuff. So, what would you expect in the very next verse? Probably not this: "Then James and John, the sons of Zebedee, came to him. 'Teacher,' they said, 'we want you to do for us whatever we ask.'"

Jesus, the one who had just announced his own death, replies, *"Seriously, guys?* What do you want me to do for you?" (Okay, we added the "Seriously, guys" part. But you can imagine what Jesus was thinking.)

James and John: "Let one of us sit at your right and the other at your left in your glory."

There it is in big, bold words: "We want to be celebrities in

God's Kingdom. We want to be known, we want to be famous, we want to be in your inner circle, we want to be part of your entourage."

Jesus: "You don't know what you are asking. Can you drink the cup I drink or be baptized with the baptism I am baptized with?"

This is a leading question. He wants their desire to be exposed even more.

James and John: "We can."

Anything you can do, we can do too. That's the language of a celebrity-seeker.

Jesus, cutting deeper into their desire than they expected, says this: "You will drink the cup I drink and be baptized with the baptism I am baptized with, but to sit at my right or left is not for me to grant. These places belong to those for whom they have been prepared."[24]

In other words, "You have no idea what you are asking because you have no idea what I'm about to face. So let me lay it out there for you: 'No, you can't!'"

Jesus now reveals the depth of his character, his mission, his way, and the way of life for all his followers (including today's pastors and churches):

> You know that those who are regarded as rulers
> of the Gentiles lord it over them, and their high
> officials exercise authority over them. Not so with
> you. Instead, whoever wants to become great among
> you must be your servant, and whoever wants to be
> first must be slave of all. For even the Son of Man did
> not come to be served, but to serve, and to give his
> life as a ransom for many.[25]

Celebrities want glory and fame. Jesus wants followers who deny glory and fame to pursue a life of service. Pastors are not celebrities, and churches are not celebrity churches. Pastors, leaders, and churches are to be known for what their Lord and Savior is known for: sacrifice for the sake of others. Service. Servanthood.

SACRIFICE FOR THE SAKE OF OTHERS

Calvin Miller tells a story in his memoir that deserves to be told here again because it is so indicative of the difference between a celebrity culture and a service-oriented culture. We pick up the story shortly after the president of the seminary where Miller was teaching has been fired.

> He was replaced within a very short time by another president, one apparently more to the trustees' liking. The new president had not been in office long when an artist was hired to paint his portrait to hang in the school rotunda, where hung all those who had previously served as president. I am not particularly opposed to having one's portrait painted to be hung in whatever worthy niche is to be found in the hallowed halls of graduate schools. But this picture always arrested my attention. Each time I passed it in the rotunda I studied it. It came to stand for all that was evil in how good men die and others come to replace them. Denominations generally put up pictures of people who run them, and often their lives are not as worthy as the lives of those uncelebrated students who pass their pictures in the hallways as they leave to take their places in the dangerous world of ministry and service.[26]

That's the first part of the story, a good setup on the author's part.

> Shortly after the new portrait went up, I happened to be at Columbia International University in South Carolina. I was passing through the hallways when I came into a large room of that school. In this room I noticed that its walls were covered with pictures of men and women. One of the university students happened to pass the room at the very moment I stood surveying those pictures.
>
> "Are these pictures of your past presidents?" I asked.
>
> "Presidents!" he almost shouted, as though I had insulted him. "Hardly presidents. These are *the important people* who have graduated from this school. Every picture in this room is not just a graduate but a martyr." . . .
>
> "You mean every person pictured here actually died for Jesus in some part of the world under some kind of persecution?"
>
> "That's exactly what I mean. Go read the tags."
>
> I did. Beside each picture was a tiny tag that told where the person had died and what was the price they had paid for their service.
>
> "This is remarkable," I said. I thought of the new picture recently hung in our rotunda. "At our school we put up pictures of our presidents."
>
> "Presidents! At our school we put up pictures of our martyrs."[27]

Ouch.

SUGGESTIONS FOR DEVELOPING
A SERVANT CULTURE

A flashy new program doesn't form a culture. Starting a compassion and justice ministry in your church will not automatically create a servant culture in the church. A servant culture develops over time. A servant culture forms when the pastor, other leaders, and the congregation take on the character of servanthood. Servanthood means surrendering our honor and time and status for the sake of someone else. (And it doesn't have to be a homeless person.)

There is an obsession in some people's minds with the homeless, or the lowest of the low. They reason that because Jesus ministered to the lepers and the poor, who were the lowest of the low in his culture (well, most people were poor, but lepers were true outcasts), we must serve the neediest of the needy in our society if we want to genuinely serve.

There's nothing wrong with serving the homeless. But let's not miss the larger point: Jesus served *everyone* on his path or in his way (to borrow language from the Good Samaritan story). His spontaneity in service annoyed his disciples, but it was *on mission* for Jesus. Service is measured by our willingness to deny ourselves for the sake of another. It is not measured by the (lowly) status of the ones we serve, but by our willingness to *surrender*—our time, resources, gifts, talents, and presence—for another.

Leaders leading others to serve

Creating a service culture in the church starts with *leaders serving*. Every pastor, minister, and director should be serving others. Over time, leaders lead others into service. Over time, service becomes a habit in the church when leaders lead others into service.

A friend of mine (Laura's) told me recently that she was walking down the hallway at her church and happened to glance into the nursery as she went by. She was surprised, and profoundly moved, to see the senior pastor holding babies. And he was good at it! In a church with a service culture, it should not be surprising to see the pastors and other leaders serving in very unassuming positions.

That's leadership.

That's *tov*.

I (Scot) have a good friend named Mike Glenn who has pastored a megachurch in Megachurchville—Nashville, Tennessee—for a long time. In his recent book, *Coffee with Mom*, Mike talks about moving his not always cooperative mother, who struggled with dementia, from Alabama to Nashville to be closer to him. I'll let him paint the picture.

> Both Jeannie, my wife, and I were working in demanding jobs. She was a triage phone nurse . . . and I was the pastor of Brentwood Baptist Church. Our boys were married and well into their careers, and Jeannie and I were new grandparents. Our lives were full and good.
>
> Then we added Mom.
>
> My family situation meant I would become Mom's primary and sole caregiver. We chose Morning Pointe in Brentwood because it was very close to our home. We could be there in minutes. It was also on my way to the church. I could stop by and have coffee with her on my way into my office.
>
> That's what I did. For four years, not every morning, but several times a week, I would stop and have coffee with Mom while she ate her breakfast. Sometimes she'd be in a good mood, and we'd laugh as we told old family stories. Other days, she'd be angry, and I'd be accused, attacked, and condemned, and yes, some days, cussed

out. Still other days, she'd be sad and unable to find a
reason to live. . . .

Unless you've been there, you don't know what it does
to your soul to see the woman who taught you about
integrity and honesty start stealing everything that wasn't
nailed down . . . and fight you if you tried to take it away.

Caring for an Alzheimer's patient means you hurt all
the time."[28]

That's what it's like to do the ordinary (yet not at all ordinary)
work of caring for someone in need. That's what it means to deny
ourselves for the sake of another. Weekly, for four years, a very
busy pastor at a big, bustling church in the buckle of the Bible Belt
got out of his car, spent time with his mother, got back in his car,
and went on with his day, tears in his eyes. That's what serving
others is like sometimes.

What Mike did set the tone for *tov* in his church. Read his
book *Coffee with Mom*, and pass it along to friends who know
what Alzheimer's does to people. Leaders set the tone for a service
culture by serving.

Stop shining the spotlight

Talking publicly about people in the church who are serving
should be prohibited—especially from the platform or pulpit or
in church-wide communications. When serving is trumpeted
from the front of the room, it's too easy for people to work for
the applause and too tempting to try to make a name for oneself
for being a selfless server. Jesus' words in Matthew 6:3—"Don't
let your left hand know what your right hand is doing"—could
be inscribed on the walls in the church offices as a reminder.
Serve and don't tell. And if you want to encourage someone who

is serving, talk to him or her in private. That's more meaningful anyway.

Avoid benevolence and paternalism

Benevolence involves the "haves" doing nice things for the "have-nots." (Remember Calvin Miller's story about the Christmas baskets.) Paternalism conveys to the powerless that the powerful are looking out for them—and don't you forget it. Both of these attitudes or mindsets—which is really what they are—must be avoided. As image-bearers of God, we are simply seeing other image-bearers of God who have a need and doing what we can to meet it in the ordinary course of life. Don't draw attention to what you're doing, and don't have a hidden agenda. As Paul cautioned the church in Rome, "Do not think of yourself more highly than you ought, but rather think of yourself with sober judgment, in accordance with the faith God has distributed to each of you."[29]

Make service a spiritual discipline

Power has a way of ruining people; success has a way of turning ministers into celebrities. Therefore, pastors must resist the pull toward celebrity—which means they must work hard to find moments of equality with others. Service can be just the right kind of leveler. Those who might otherwise be seen as high-status people in the church—pastors, ministry leaders, prominent parishioners—should *turn service into a spiritual discipline.* Pastors must be accessible. The less accessible the pastor, the greater the chance of a celebrity mindset taking hold and service losing its grip. Pastors who are too busy to pastor the people in their church, who are too detached to be spoken to, who are too inaccessible to receive emails and text messages, are too big for their britches. What does it mean to be a *pastor* if one has no connection to the people?

Share the pulpit

More pastors, especially those who are too big for their britches, need to share the pulpit as a means of de-elevating their status. The most powerful moment for power-driven pastors is the sermon. Pastors can become quite protective of the pulpit and jealous of others who are skilled and effective in preaching. A simple way to combat prideful tendencies is to make room for others to preach and teach in the church. Here's a fact: Most preachers are average (that's what average means), but most preachers think they are above average. It reminds me of a quip I once heard about college professors: "When more than 90 percent of faculty members rate themselves as above-average teachers, and two-thirds rate themselves among the top quarter, the outlook for much improvement in teaching seems less than promising."[30] If it's true with college professors, it's even more true with preachers. Sharing the pulpit or hosting speakers for a conference is a good way for a pastor to remind himself that it's not all about *him*, a good way to develop the teaching gift in others, and a surefire step toward creating a servanthood mentality.

Develop the discipline of losing arguments

Not long ago, a student of mine—a fine young pastor—asked me how he could avoid "becoming like Pastor X" when he was older. He was growing in success and admitted that he had it within him to become that kind of person. I advocated the discipline of losing arguments. This is how our conversation went:

> Me: Do you ever lose any decisions with your elders,
>   deacons, and leaders?
> Him: Not really.
> Me: You need to lose some.

Him: What do you mean?

Me: Not all decisions are important. In a discussion where you are about 60 percent convinced, intentionally side with the 40 percent.

Him: Why?

Me: Because when your leaders see that you don't have to win every single battle, they will see that the church matters more than you.

The goal is to create a culture within leadership that says, "*We* matter more than *I* matter." That mindset can breed an entire culture of service to one another.

Lead with transparency

A servant culture coalesces around *transparency*. David Fitch, my friend and colleague at Northern Seminary, has said in the presence of our African American and female colleagues, "If I ever say anything that you find racist or sexist, call me on it right then."

When he told me one time that he'd been called on it, I asked him, "What did you say?"

"I submit and I apologize!"

Anyone who knows David Fitch knows he loves to say, "I submit," so there's a personality aura surrounding such comments, but David pastors along with his professoring, and he seeks to form transparency in his church culture, as well. Transparency with one another is a form of serving one another.

In the Circle of *Tov*, a service culture forms at such a deep level that anything smacking of celebrity gets a quick smackdown.

TOV CHURCHES NURTURE CHRISTLIKENESS

IN THE CIRCLE OF *TOV*, when we practice the habits of empathy and compassion, extending grace, putting people first, telling the truth, promoting justice, and serving others, *tov* emerges in the culture and we all become more like Christ. Goodness (*tov*) becomes an agent that influences every aspect of our lives. And the more we practice *tov*, the more the culture becomes *tov* . . . and round and round the circle of goodness we go! But when churches become businesses, corporations, or institutions, pastors cease to be pastors, churches cease to be churches, and the culture in the church becomes toxic, not *tov*.

Something radical has seeped into the church in the last fifty years. The American meritocracy has reshaped pastors and churches, and a new culture has taken root, based on achievement and accomplishment rather than holiness and Christlikeness. This new culture is not all bad, by any means, but it must be seen for what it is, and also for its limitations. Let's begin by defining what it means to say that an achievement and accomplishment culture has taken root.

THE RISE OF AN ACHIEVEMENT
AND ACCOMPLISHMENT CULTURE

In a society focused on achievement and accomplishment, the challenge we face in the church is to avoid being squeezed into that mold and shaped in that image. Achievement and accomplishment are two foundational pillars of a meritocracy, which refers to power (-*cracy* from the Greek *kratos*) based on merit—that is, based on value, worth, or what we deserve or earn. For insight to the implications of a meritocracy, we again turn to David Brooks, one of our society's great cultural observers.

> The meritocracy is the most self-confident moral system
> in the world today. It's so engrossing and seems so natural
> that we're not even aware of how it encourages a certain
> economic vocabulary about noneconomic things.[1]

What Brooks says next is stunning and penetrating to the core.

> Words change their meaning. "Character" is no longer
> a moral quality oriented around love, service, and
> care, but *a set of workplace traits organized around grit,*
> *productivity, and self-discipline.*[2]

Community, too, is relabeled:

> The meritocracy defines "community" as *a mass of talented*
> *individuals competing with one another.* It organizes society

into an endless set of outer and inner rings, with high achievers at the Davos center and everybody else arrayed across the wider rings toward the edge. While it pretends not to, it subliminally sends the message that those who are smarter and more accomplished are actually worth more than those who are not.

The meritocracy's soul-flattening influence is survivable if you have your own competing moral system that exists in you alongside it, but if you have no competing value system, the meritocracy swallows you whole.[3]

Remember what Brooks said earlier: "Never underestimate the power of the environment you work in to gradually transform who you are."[4]

Churches today have been so greatly influenced by meritocracy, by the achievement and accomplishment culture of the business world, that they now define *pastor* with business-culture terms instead of biblical terms. In business terms, a pastor is a "leader," and *leader* is defined by the meritocratic system of American culture. But when pastors are defined primarily as *leaders*—or *entrepreneurs* or *visionaries*—they've already ceased to be pastors in any biblical sense. Further, when the church becomes an *institution* or an *organization*—or worse, a *corporation*—it ceases to be a church (that is, a vital part of the body of Christ). Moreover, "pastor as leader" blurs the lines of headship in the church, and people begin to lose sight of the church's one true and only head, Jesus Christ.

LEADERS AND THE BUSINESS WORLD

Here's what I (Scot) observed as the term *leader* began to take hold in the church, with *leadership* taking its definition from the business world.

1. Pastors became leaders, entrepreneurs, or visionaries—
   and wealthy ones at that, in some cases.
2. The pastor's preparation no longer required seminary,
   the foundation for most pastors for centuries. When
   seminary is not the pathway to preparation, something
   else will take its place. Often enough it's the business
   world, sometimes euphemized as "experience."
3. The church was now referred to as an *organization* rather
   than an *organism*. The former is a human institution,
   whereas the latter represents the living body of Christ.
4. The Bible became a source for finding leadership
   principles—Moses as a leader, Joshua as a leader, Ezekiel
   as a . . . nope, no one ever went to him for leadership.
5. The church began producing a product, which naturally
   led to positioning, advertising, and promoting the
   product.
6. The church now needed a vision statement and a
   mission statement, both terms that came out of "best
   practices" in the business world. This led to churches
   "branding" themselves, which is as businessy a term as
   you can find.
7. Churches began to do customer satisfaction surveys. Oh,
   would the Old Testament prophets have a field day here.
   Their mission seemed to be customer *dissatisfaction* or
   discomfort.
8. The bottom line (another business term) was that the
   church now needed a bottom line, typically measured by
   butts in the pews, "giving units," or dollars contributed.

A leadership culture turns the church into an organization, governed by a set of management principles. It turns pastors into leaders whose primary aim is the success of the organization—based in some way on achievable metrics. The more ambitious the leader and the more narcissistic the leader, the less of a church the church becomes. All this has a huge impact on culture formation in the church.

TWO PASTOR MODELS, TWO CHURCH CULTURES

When Willow Creek posted a job description for Bill Hybels's replacement, I (Scot) pasted it into a Word Cloud—a popular way to visualize the most frequently used words in a written communication. The results amazed me. As someone who teaches pastors and future pastors, I decided to gather major Bible passages about pastoring or shepherding, paste them into another Word Cloud, and compare those results with the Willow Creek job description. Seen side-by-side, the two Word Clouds stand as a stark illustration of what is happening in our churches.

Leadership has long been a Willow Creek buzzword. This is borne out by the job description they posted online, in which *leader* was the dominant word.[5] The words *lead, leader, leading,* or *leadership* appear *thirty-two* times in defining what Willow Creek was looking for in its next senior pastor.

"He or she will be a proven 'leader of leaders' who can motivate and inspire high-capacity men and women to use their gifts to further the vision."

"[The senior pastor will] put emphasis on leadership development, individually modeling this at the highest levels."

"We have a strong preference toward leaders with multi-site or complex organizational experience."

"When you look in the rearview mirror of this leader's life, you see growing organizations."[6]

WORD CLOUD FOR WILLOW CREEK
JOB DESCRIPTION

The job description included plenty of references to *organization*, *vision*, *mission*, and *strategy*, too. Willow Creek said it wanted its next leader to have "life experience in connecting with . . . people who have *outwardly made it in life* but are seeking significance."[7] Thus interpreted: Jesus and the apostles need not apply. Or maybe we should rethink the pastor-as-CEO concept altogether.

**WORD CLOUD FOR BIBLE PASSAGES ABOUT
PASTORING OR SHEPHERDING**

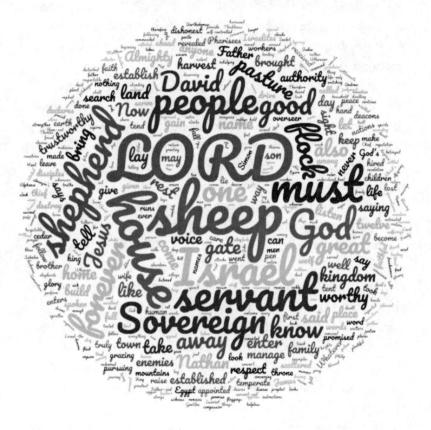

The late Eugene Peterson, well-known translator of *The Message* and author of some of the finest books ever written for pastors, staunchly resisted the invasion of a business culture into the lifeblood of the church. He was particularly concerned that pastors were becoming leaders, entrepreneurs, and managers rather than preserving their calling as *spiritual directors* of the faith community. Most of Peterson's books address in some way the need for spiritual formation and spiritual direction, and he seemed to always take issue with the newfangled development of pastors as leaders. He defined the three most important pastoral acts as "praying, reading Scripture, and giving spiritual direction."[8] I've never heard a pastor who focuses on the pastor as leader say anything like this. Ever.

Take another look at the Word Clouds. Two pastors, one focused on leadership principles and the other focused on spiritual formation. Two cultures forming around two separate images. One will become *tov* (with all its attributes), and the other will become toxic (and it will not surprise anyone when people are treated abusively and with disrespect).

I (Scot) watched this shift happen, from pastors as pastors and spiritual directors to pastors as leaders and entrepreneurs, and I can illustrate it through personal history. When I was young, pastors and parents and Sunday school teachers challenged young males (mostly) to give their lives to Christ and put it all on the altar. From this point there developed a ranking of worthy callings, defined by perceived levels of zeal more than hierarchy. However it happened, the highest rank was to be a missionary, the second level was to be an evangelist, and the third was to be a pastor. Nobody, and I mean not even one, ever talked about surrendering their life to become a *leader*.

When leadership became a craze in the 1980s and 1990s, it irritated many in the church, but the irritated ones lost. I, too, chafed against the idea, and when I was asked one time to write a short essay on leadership, I wrote it on "followership" instead. In an effort to subvert the whole notion of church leadership, I pointed out that Jesus never said to anyone, "Come, become a leader." He said, "Come, follow me." He wanted followers, not leaders. Hence, followership.

Let's push this a little further: Do you know how many times Jesus talked about people becoming leaders? Not once. Do you know how many times Paul uses the term *leader*? A handful, and that's being generous. Look them up in your Bible: The term *prohistemi* (which means to stand in front) refers to elders or what we would call church leaders (Romans 12:8; 1 Thessalonians 5:12; 1 Timothy 5:17), seemingly to all Christians "leading" in good works (Titus 3:8, 14), and to fathers leading their families (1 Timothy 3:4, 12).

It might be fair to say that what the church needs are not pastor-leaders but pastors who will shepherd under the Great Shepherd, Jesus. Yes, pastors provide some leadership, but they should be leading toward spiritual formation. My concern, borne out by experience, is that if we start calling our pastors "leaders," we run the risk of their losing contact with the pastoral calling and starting to shape the culture toward an institution or business run by a CEO.

Back on the path now. In the 1980s and 1990s we had a sudden influx of church leadership magazines, church leadership conferences, and trend-setting churches like Willow Creek, and North Point in Atlanta, gaining prominence. It all culminated in a sense at Willow Creek's Global Leadership Summit where *everyone* was invited to attend and learn how to "lead where you are." Summit attenders were encouraged to read Bill Hybels's leadership books, churches were drawn into the Willow Creek Association, and it all further enhanced Willow Creek's culture of leadership.

We need leaders in the church, but here's the issue: When a young person, male or female, wants to become a leader or an "influencer" (another term being bandied about today) in the church, it connotes a self-centered emphasis on that person's role and identity. Choosing to label oneself as a leader creates a certain expectation of a job description and a measure of achievement and accomplishment.

Think of it this way. There's a reason the Bible refers to Jesus as Messiah, Lord, and Savior, but not Leader. It has to do with his preeminent headship. There's a reason the Bible refers to Peter, James, and John as disciples and apostles, but not leaders. It has to do with their relationship with and commissioning by Jesus. Yes, Jesus was a leader, but he was also Messiah (which swallows up and redefines leadership). Sure, Peter, James, and John were leaders, but they were foremost apostles (which swallows up and redefines their leadership).

The vast majority of discussions about church leadership draw their core principles from the business world, and business leaders are the core for defining the role of leaders in the church. Just pick up one of the many books about church leaders, and you will notice the predominance of business leadership models and principles and a superficial use of the Bible. Simply stated, the Bible doesn't use the term *leader* the way we use it today. Again, we need leaders, but perhaps the better word is *pastor*—and let the parameters of that term define what a leader is!

Instead of focusing on "leadership development," we should be focusing on Christ and Christ alone as our model, and Christlikeness as the core identity of *every* Christian—yes, including Christian pastors. The role of the pastor, then, is to mentor people into Christlikeness.

SO, WHAT IS A PASTOR?

We'll let a pastor have the first word—Eugene Peterson, a pastor who was seen by many as a pastor of pastors. In his beautiful memoir, *The Pastor*, Peterson addresses the invasion of an achievement and accomplishment culture into the church.

In the process of realizing my vocational identity as pastor, I couldn't help observing that there was a great deal of confusion and dissatisfaction all around me with pastoral identity. Many pastors, disappointed or disillusioned with their congregations, defect after a few years and find more congenial work. And many congregations, disappointed or disillusioned with their pastors, dismiss them and look for pastors more to their liking. In the fifty years that I have lived the vocation of pastor, these defections and dismissals have reached epidemic proportions in every branch and form of church.

I wonder if at the root of the defection is a cultural assumption that all leaders are people who "get things done," and "make things happen." That is certainly true of the primary leadership models that seep into our awareness from the culture—politicians, businessmen, advertisers, publicists, celebrities, and athletes. But while being a pastor certainly has some of these components, the pervasive element in our two-thousand-year pastoral tradition is not someone who "gets things done" but rather the person placed in the community to pay attention and call attention to "what is going on right now" between men and women, with one another and with God—this kingdom of God that is primarily local, relentlessly personal, and prayerful "without ceasing."[9]

If we want to form a *tov* culture in the church, one that can heal the wounded, we need to operate according to God's design, not the latest leadership model. Here is God's design for a pastor: *A pastor is someone called to nurture Christoformity in himself or herself and in others.*

THE CIRCLE OF *TOV*
Nurturing Habits of Goodness

Nurture Christlikeness
Resist the leader culture

Nurture empathy
Resist a narcissist's culture

Nurture service
Resist the celebrity culture

TOV

Nurture grace
Resist a fear culture

Nurture justice
Resist the loyalty culture

Put people first
Resist institution creep

Tell the truth
Resist false narratives
Know Yom Kippur
Form a truth-telling culture

The word *Christoformity* means "to be conformed to Christ." In other words, it is Christlikeness. Pastors, by definition, pastor from their own personal Christoformity.[10] No pastor is perfect, that's for sure, but pastors are to be mature enough Christians to be able to mentor others into Christlikeness as they are moving into Christlikeness themselves. We are in this together.

The pastor's goal is to help each person he or she shepherds become more like Jesus. That's what pastoring is all about. That's what is so egregious about the abuse of women and children in the church, the abuse of power in the church, and false narratives in the church.

It is a sad fact that many pastors (and therefore many congregants) think the primary purpose of Sunday mornings is to preach (or listen to) a sermon. Preaching is part of the purpose, but when it becomes the central or all-encompassing purpose, Sunday mornings become little more than "come hear me preach." A "come hear me preach" culture is not *tov*. I'm not knocking preaching, but I am knocking the idea of a pastor as primarily a preacher. Preaching is only one dimension of a comprehensive task.

I (Laura) admit to being guilty of this obsession with preaching. Too often, Mark and I would skip Saturday evening services at Willow Creek because we "didn't like listening to this week's speaker." Or maybe the Cubs were playing and we couldn't possibly miss the Cubs because they might clinch a playoff berth. (Go Cubs.) Or our neighbors were biking to dinner and the weather was so nice and we didn't want to miss the fun. We had FOMO (fear of missing out). We had endless excuses is what we had. But the problem remained: We could not motivate ourselves to attend church, most often blaming the Person Who Would Be Preaching. The primary purpose of my church attendance had become to Listen to the Speaker. And maybe if we were lucky that week, we would like the worship! Mark was more intentional about engaging with our community, which seems like an actual need and far more appropriate than my hyperfocus on the speaker. But if our friends weren't there, we felt it was a total miss. We had become consumers and evaluators, and we were in the deepest of ruts, dreading Saturday evenings for many, many weeks.

I have no doubt that many folks faithfully attend Willow Creek and other megachurches each week and do not share my hyperfocus on the speaker. I do not blame Willow Creek for the rut I landed in. But I do believe our move to a different church culture awakened my soul to purer purposes for church attendance. When we began attending Church of the Redeemer, we slowly grew in our understanding that the purpose of church is not the preacher. We now follow the church calendar, which includes weeks for

Lent and Easter and Pentecost and Advent and Ordinary Time. But they are not "themes" or "series." As Jay, our pastor, says, they offer us the healing arc of liturgical rhythm. Each Sunday, there is the faithfully simple reading of liturgy from the Old Testament, followed by a Psalm, an Epistle reading, and a reading from one of the four Gospels. There is worship and a message—but not as the centerpiece—followed by the recitation of the Nicene Creed, corporate prayer, confession of sin, and passing the peace, all culminating in Communion—that is, remembering the sacrifice of Christ on our behalf.

If the service "builds" to anything, it is our church family taking and receiving the Lord's Supper together. It is the children returning from their Sunday school classes and joining their parents; it is families going forward together to receive the bread and wine or a tender blessing.

"Come," Jay often says before he breaks the Communion bread. "Just come as you are."

We receive Communion together as a family, as families did together in the first century and early church, with a commitment to raise children in the faith of their parents. It is our pastor placing the Bread of Life in our hands, looking each congregant in the eye, and telling us by name that Jesus' body is broken for us. (There is something so moving about those words week after week.) It is a volunteer like Lesley or Carol or Al looking each of us in the eye, giving us the Cup of Salvation, reminding us that Jesus died for us.

As a side note, our church attendance has become a lot more consistent. We've come to understand that "church" is not an event, and it is not about the pastor's sermon. Church attendance is about joining a community of believers and being nurtured in the faith. Church is about soul work and confession of sin. Church is about relationships and community—which take time to build. Church is about knowing and being known, loving and being loved, serving and being served. I believe our attendance is regular now because we're no longer focused on hearing a certain preacher. Most weeks, we don't even know who is preaching, and it is not the most important thing. We love our pastor because he is gentle and humble, he knows our names, and he is happy to see us, not because he's a good speaker (though he is).

To pastor means to nurture both individuals and congregations spiritually. Pastors are designed for what used to be called "the cure of souls" and what Eugene Peterson referred to as "the ministry of small talk."[11] It's about ordinary life. In another context, Peterson observed that "pastoral theology, as Paul lives and writes it, is relational—persons are involved as persons-in-relationship."[12]

Paul himself speaks of "the daily burden of my concern for all the churches."[13] Speaking to the elders of the church at Ephesus, Paul says, "Remember the three years I was with you—my constant watch and care over you night and day, and my many tears for you.[14] Paul was vulnerable: He "had no peace of mind" when Titus was late in arriving at Troas.[15] And he wanted the Corinthians to open their hearts to him.[16] The pastor's emotions are influenced by how the people are growing in Christ. We could go on.

WHAT IS A CHURCH?

The dangers of viewing a church as an organization are similar to the dangers of pastors as leaders. The words matter. A church is not a business, it isn't producing a product, and it doesn't gauge success based on measurables. A church is a local community of believers who are striving to be like Christ, both as a congregation and as individuals. Its leadership is peculiar because churches don't function based on hierarchies and reporting relationships.

They function based on the interdependence of gifted individuals working together to honor, worship, and serve God, under the exclusive headship of Jesus Christ, and empowered and inspired by the Holy Spirit.

That the church calls its Lord *Jesus Christ*—combining Hebrew and Greek words into an English name—is a clue to what the church is meant to be. *Jesus* derives from the Hebrew name *Yehoshua* (which could also be translated Joshua), which means God delivers, saves, rescues. *Christ* derives from a Greek translation of the Hebrew *Mashiach* (also where we get the word *Messiah*), which means "anointed one." The church, then, declares that we are following Israel's God, who, true to his covenant promise, sent his Son, the one anointed to redeem his people. As such, the church fulfills Israel's story. Our allegiance to Jesus Christ establishes our identity, tells us how we are to live, points us in the direction we should go, and fills us with memories and hopes.

Church as a people, not an organization, business, or enterprise, is the means by which other people are enfolded into God's family. Our purpose is redemptive and restorative, not for profit, position, or power. Those who align themselves under the headship of Jesus as Lord identify with the redemptive work of salvation accomplished by Jesus on the cross (and brought to fulfillment by his resurrection and ascension), and they are brought into restored relationship with "the God who saves." Jesus releases us from our sins, rescues us from Satan's clutches, and liberates us from the systemic evil at work in the world. There is no business model that covers this.

God's covenant is with Israel, but his people are no longer *just* Israel. We (the church) have been grafted in.[17] To the church's shame, it has often spoken as if God's covenant with Israel is a thing of the past, but no one who embraces Jesus as Lord can erase God's covenant history with Israel. Their story is our story. That said, the genius of the church is the expansion to include Gentiles, those who were formerly outside the covenant and strangers to the promises. The church is a multiethnic, multinational, multiracial—and thus multicultural—community of redeemed people under one King, Jesus.

The gospel invades our achievement-oriented, meritocratic world—where success is measured by accomplishments and numbers—and it says *no, no, no*. It says success is not measured by numbers. It says pastors and churches have an entirely different agenda—namely, helping others grow in Christlikeness. That is a lifelong process and pursuit, and we are all at different points along the way. It is a process based on love, not on business management or leadership principles.

Notice these words from the apostle John:

God is love, and all who live in love live in God, and God lives in them. And as we live in God, our love grows more perfect. So we will not be afraid on the day of judgment, but we can face him with confidence *because we live like Jesus* here in this world.

Such love has no fear, because perfect love expels all fear. If we are afraid, it is for fear of punishment, and this shows that we have not fully experienced his perfect love.[18]

SUCCESS REDEFINED

The pastor's calling and the church's calling are to nurture people into Christoformity—to nurture people into *tov*. God is good, Christ is good, and to be like Christ is to be *tov*. We have come full circle now. The entire Circle of *Tov* is swallowed up and comprehensively expressed by Christlikeness.

Growing in Christlikeness stands in stark contrast to an

achievement culture measured by numbers, power, prestige, and money. It is a constant temptation for churches and pastors to be drawn away from a Christlike culture and sucked into the culture of the world.

In a Christlike culture of *tov*, something completely different from the culture of the world pervades, something so upside down and so backwards it is nothing less than stunning. Jesus calls people to follow him to the cross, and the apostle Paul uses that cross-bearing life to redefine true success:

> In your relationships with one another, have the same mindset as Christ Jesus:
>
> > Who, being in very nature God,
> > > did not consider equality with God something to be
> > > used to his own advantage;
> > rather, he made himself nothing
> > > by taking the nature of a servant,
> > > being made in human likeness.
> > And being found in appearance as a man,
> > > he humbled himself
> > > by becoming obedient to death—
> > > > even death on a cross!
>
> > Therefore God exalted him to the highest place
> > > and gave him the name that is above every name,
> > that at the name of Jesus every knee should bow,
> > > in heaven and on earth and under the earth,
> > and every tongue acknowledge that Jesus Christ is Lord,
> > > to the glory of God the Father.[19]

The way of Jesus is the cross-bearing life. Therefore, the way of those in union with Jesus, those who want to follow Jesus, is also the cross-bearing life. The cross-bearing life, or what we're call-ing Christoformity, is a life surrendered to Jesus for the sake of others. This is the *tov* culture we are called to establish, stimulate, and nurture.

A *tov* church culture embraces this pursuit, this calling, for its pastors and its people. *Tov* summons pastors—get a good grip on this—to pastor the people they have, not the people they don't have. Growth, in all its aspects, is the work of the Holy Spirit, not the work of the pastor, the leaders, or the church.

Some pastors, church leaders, and congregations are intoxi-cated by numbers, and they measure themselves against others. But there is only one church. Growth is good, but the purpose of the church is not numerical growth or filling seats. The purpose of the church is conformity to Christ. That is the sum total of God's plan. Read Paul's words to the Romans: "For God knew his people in advance, and he chose them to become like his Son."[20] There in simple language is the entire mission of the church and its pastors: to become like Christ and nurture others to become like Christ.

We help one another become more like Jesus through the exer-cise of spiritual gifts, as each person contributes to the whole and to one another.[21] As such, we learn to put away sinful habits, which the Bible calls the flesh, and put on the habits of *tov*, which Paul calls the fruit of the Spirit.[22]

A word about spiritual gifts and the role of every person in everyday ministry in a church called *tov*: Every person is a minis-ter, every person is gifted by the Holy Spirit, and everyone has an ongoing ministry. That ministry is what God equips each person to do. Teresa Morgan, a brilliant professor at Oxford University of the classical worlds of Greece and Rome and a priest in the Church of England, tells us how she learned to see her life as an exercise in the gifts God had given her:

I didn't see myself as a priest in my parish and a lecturer at work, but as living one life of faith in several places. Bit by bit, a few ideas began to germinate about how someone might be a priest in and for their working community.

It would not involve talking about religion very much, unless other people wanted to. Most of my colleagues were not religious, or were religious but not Christian. I respected them personally; I respected their religious and other commitments; I did not plan to give them indigestion by telling them over lunch what I thought they ought to believe. It seemed to me that ministering at work should be more about "showing" than "telling."

Day by day, I would try to be attentive to the people around me, especially if they were in need of practical help, encouragement or just a listening ear. I would speak out and act, if necessary, against inequality, unkindness or injustice. I would try to live in harmony with my colleagues and students, and to foster forgiveness and reconciliation whenever we fell out. I would look for ways of teaching, writing, taking part in meetings or doing routine administration that made my institution a more loving, peaceful, joyful place, and helped it share those qualities with the wider world. Finally, I would say every day to God, "Not my will but yours be done," and wait and see what God did with my obedience.[23]

Sounds like a plan for *tov*!

What happens in our churches if we focus on the sorts of goals the apostle Paul focused on in his churches? What happens when we measure success by Christlikeness? What happens to our boards of elders and deacons and leaders? What happens to our programming and our preaching and our music? What happens when we reimagine church as a school for sinners who are gradually learning the way of Christ?

No church is perfect, we all know that. Those looking for the perfect church, even a church that flourishes into the expectations above, will quickly be disappointed. Nevertheless, every church should be on the journey toward becoming a church called *tov*. The Circle of *Tov* expresses some of the major biblical themes that our churches need today.

WHAT CAN WE DO?

This question may have been on your mind since the beginning of this book: *What can we do?* For a basic framework, we turn to Patrick Keifert and Wesley Granberg-Michaelson, two experts on church change who have learned and refined their approach through decades of working with congregations to transform their cultures.[24] Their suggestions are fivefold, and we have adopted, adapted, and adjusted them toward our Circle of *Tov*.

First, express the mission of God for your church as *tov*, which is characterized perfectly in working together to become more like Jesus.

Second, open space for the creative work of God's Spirit to lead your church into *tov*, and avoid programming, governing, and constraining this creative work of God's Spirit.

Third, at all levels become available to the revealing discernment of the Holy Spirit for how *tov* can take root in your church.

Fourth, *dwell* in the Word. That is, routinely read the Word together and let the Word speak about how God is leading you toward *tov*.

Fifth, cooperate with other churches in the process of eradicating a toxic culture and forming your church into a church called *tov*.[25]

A CLOSING PRAYER

Father of All Mercy,

You know the hearts and minds and acts of all your people.

You know all and you reveal your truth in Christ.

Grant to us, your people, including the pastors and churches mentioned in this book, to know the truth of the gospel (which unmasks our pretenses, our quest for power, and our sins) and to know the truth of your grace, which transforms us into Christlikeness.

Grant further, O Lord, the rich graces of reconciliation between those on opposing sides of these devastating events in churches.

Grant this so that we may live in the light, knowing the graces of your forgiveness and power and walking in the way that brings you all the glory.

Through Him who lives with you, the Holy Spirit, one God, now and forever.

Amen.

ACKNOWLEDGMENTS

First and foremost, we honor the courageous women of Willow: Vonda Dyer, Keri Ladouceur, Nancy Beach, Nancy Ortberg, Julia Williams, Moe Girkins, Pat Baranowski, and others who remain unnamed. We also honor Leanne Mellado, Jimmy Mellado, and Betty Schmidt.

To Steve and Sarah Carter, who gave up everything to do what is right: It wasn't easy. It still isn't easy. We hope the words in this book offer encouragement. Your sacrifice is seen. We are so grateful to know you.

A book like this could not have been written without an abundance of support.

Kris, you were with us every step, offering advice, overhearing a thousand and one conversations, and answering question after question as we continually sought your expertise as a clinical psychologist. Your persistent defense of women and perception of abusive powers made every page of this book better.

Mark, you were also with us every step and for those thousand and one conversations. Your thought-provoking questions led to deeper and more meaningful ideas that we developed in this book. As I wrote at our kitchen table almost the entire summer of 2019, you would walk by and become part of yet another chapter, sometimes by name but always in wisdom.

Mike Breaux, you offered most valuable advice and insights upon reading the manuscript. Thank you for the wisdom you shared. The book is better because you read it and gave honest feedback.

I (Laura) experienced devastating relational loss months after the Willow Creek story became public. Becki Bellito, Bryna Williamson, and Ruth Grigson, your friendship was and is a refuge. To Amanda Vanecko and Jaime Patrick, thank you. And to Lori Johnson and Donna Claffey, thank you for listening with endless patience.

The professionalism of journalists Manya Brachear Pashman and Bob Smietana was both encouraging and inspiring. You deserve the credit for breaking open the Willow Creek story.

Church of the Redeemer, thank you for creating a culture of goodness in which we delight.

To Joel Weber and Mitch Little: Thank you for your friendship, your wisdom, and your advice for this book.

I (Scot) cannot begin to recall the number of friends with whom I have had conversations about church culture, about *tov*, about leaders, and about what went wrong and why. Many of my students have asked me questions that made me think about this topic in ways I was reluctant to explore, and they have made the book better. Some of my students have been fierce defenders of what is right and have encouraged me over and over. My colleague David Fitch has crabbed about megachurches for years in my hearing. Crabbing aside, he's one of the few who comprehend the complexity and (at times) corruption of what is happening in America's megachurches. Thanks also to Ryan Mahoney and Scott Bryant, who talked to me a few times about Harvest Bible Chapel. You are not alone.

Some cannot go on record by name, but their input both broadened and deepened our understanding. From two, I learned far more than I wanted to know.

Thanks to Diane Chandler, who gave me ideas by which to process church culture breakdown.

We appreciate our wonderful editorial team at Tyndale: Jon Farrar, Jan Long Harris, and Jillian Schlossberg. Dave Lindstedt, you handled us with marvelous care and edited as well as you listened.

Finally, we honor you who were wounded in the process of your resistance.

NOTES

FOREWORD BY TISH HARRISON WARREN

1. *Glory Descending: Michael Ramsey and His Writings*, ed. Douglas Dales et al. (Grand Rapids: Eerdmans, 2005), 102.
2. Jacques Ellul, *Money and Power*, trans. LaVonne Neff (Eugene, OR: Wipf and Stock, 2009), 18.

INTRODUCTION: WHERE WE FIND OURSELVES

1. Manya Brachear Pashman and Jeff Coen, "After Years of Inquiries, Willow Creek Pastor Denies Misconduct Allegations," *Chicago Tribune*, March 23, 2018, www.chicagotribune.com/news/local/breaking/ct-met-willow-creek -pastor-20171220-story.html.
2. Pashman and Coen, "After Years of Inquiries."
3. Pashman and Coen, "After Years of Inquiries."
4. Pashman and Coen, "After Years of Inquiries."
5. Scot McKnight, "About Willow Creek: What Do I Think?" *Jesus Creed* (blog), June 27, 2018, https://www.patheos.com/blogs/jesuscreed/2018/06/27/about -willow-creek-what-do-i-think.
6. Harvest Bible Chapel, "November 3, 2019 Elder Update," www .harvestbiblechapel.org/2019/11/03/november-3-2019-elder-update.
7. Kate Shellnutt, "Sovereign Grace Calls Outside Investigation 'Impossible,'" *Christianity Today*, April 18, 2019, https://www.christianitytoday.com/news /2019/april/sovereign-grace-churches-sgc-sgm-independent-investigation-.html.
8. See Alex Johnson, "Tennessee Pastor Andy Savage Resigns Weeks after Admitting 'Sexual Incident' with Minor," NBC News, March 20, 2018, https:// www.nbcnews.com/storyline/sexual-misconduct/tennessee-pastor-andy -savage-resigns-weeks-after-admitting-sexual-incident-n858541; and Leonardo Blair, "Megachurch Pastor Resigns over Allegations of Sex with 18-Year-Old Members of Youth Group 17 Years Ago," *Christian Post*, November 29, 2019, https://www.christianpost.com/news/megachurch-pastor-resigns-over -allegations-of-sex-with-18-year-old-members-youth-group.html.

9. Sarah Pulliam Bailey, "Mark Driscoll Removed from the Acts 29 Church Planting Network He Helped Found," *Washington Post*, August 8, 2014, https://www.washingtonpost.com/national/religion/mark-driscoll-removed-from-the-acts-29-church-planting-network-he-helped-found/2014/08/08/e8e6137c-1f41-11e4-9b6c-12e30cbe86a3_story.html.

10. Plaintiff's Amended Original Complaint and Jury Demand, *Jane Roe v. Leighton Paige Patterson and Southwestern Baptist Theological Seminary*, Civil No. 4:19-cv-00179-ALM-KPJ, document 8, filed 5/22/19, page 8 of 34, PageID#: 77, item 25, https://baptistblog.files.wordpress.com/2019/06/amended-complaint.pdf.

11. Matthew 10:5-6, NIV

12. Matthew 9:36, NIV

13. Matthew 9:37-38

14. Genesis 1:4, 10, 12, 18, 21, 25

15. Genesis 1:31, NIV

CHAPTER 1: EVERY CHURCH IS A CULTURE

1. David Brooks, *The Second Mountain: The Quest for a Moral Life* (New York: Random House, 2019), 22.

2. David Brooks, *Second Mountain*, xxxi.

3. Andy Crouch, *Culture Making: Recovering Our Creative Calling* (Downers Grove, IL: IVP, 2008), 23. Italics added.

4. Crouch, *Culture Making*, 69. Italics added.

5. "Uncovering and Facing Spiritual Abuse," The Barnabas Ministry, 2006, www.barnabasministry.com/recovery-uncovering.html.

6. Matthew 12:33

7. Matthew 12:34

8. Matthew 12:35

9. Galatians 5:19, 22, NIV

CHAPTER 2: EARLY WARNING SIGNS OF A TOXIC CULTURE

1. Luke 4:18-19, NIV

2. "Narcissistic Personality Disorder," Mayo Clinic, www.mayoclinic.org/diseases-conditions/narcissistic-personality-disorder/symptoms-causes/syc-20366662.

3. "Narcissistic Personality Disorder," Mayo Clinic.

4. Proverbs 27:6

5. James C. Galvin, *Willow Creek Governance Review, 2014–2018*, April 14, 2019: 5, https://gallery.mailchimp.com/dfd0f4e0c107728235d2ff080/files/6d3bafc4-0b43-450c-8e1e-4eb1c80771e2/Report_on_Governance_Review_2014_2018_FINAL.pdf.

6. Ronald M. Enroth, *Churches That Abuse* (Grand Rapids: Zondervan, 1992), 202–203.

7. Galvin, *Willow Creek Governance Review*, 3, 5.

8. Galvin, *Willow Creek Governance Review*, 3–5.

9. Galvin, *Willow Creek Governance Review*, 4.

10. Galvin, *Willow Creek Governance Review*, 5.

11. Julie Roys, "Hard Times at Harvest," *World* magazine, December 13, 2018, https://world.wng.org/2018/12/hard_times_at_harvest.

12. "James MacDonald Harvest Bible Chapel Excommunication," Internet Archive, September 19, 2013, https://archive.org/details /JamesMacDonaldHarvestBibleChapel, 3:28–3:33.

13. Roys, "Hard Times at Harvest."

14. Roys, "Hard Times at Harvest."

15. Anthony Everitt, *The Rise of Athens* (New York: Random House, 2016), 68.

16. Ellen F. Davis, *Proverbs, Ecclesiastes, and the Song of Songs* (Louisville, KY: Westminster John Knox, 2000), 27.

17. Ronald Enroth, *Churches That Abuse* (Grand Rapids: Zondervan, 1992), 196.

18. Jerry Useem, "Power Causes Brain Damage," *The Atlantic*, July/August 2017, www.theatlantic.com/magazine/archive/2017/07/power-causes-brain -damage/528711.

19. David Owen and Jonathan Davidson, "Hubris Syndrome: An Acquired Personality Disorder? A Study of US Presidents and UK Prime Ministers over the Last 100 Years," *Brain* 132, no. 5, May 2009, 1396–1406, https://academic .oup.com/brain/article/132/5/1396/354862.

20. Owen and Davidson, "Hubris Syndrome."

21. From the product description on https://bakerbookhouse.com/products/what -do-they-hear-bridging-the-gap-between-pulpit-pew-9780687642052.

22. Bill Hybels, *Axiom: Powerful Leadership Proverbs* (Grand Rapids: Zondervan, 2008), 145.

23. Hybels, *Axiom*, 145–146.

24. Jill Monaco, "Detoxing after Working at Harvest Bible Chapel," https:// jillmonaco.com/detoxing-after-working-at-harvest-bible-chapel.

CHAPTER 3: HOW TOXIC CULTURES RESPOND TO CRITICISM

1. Bob Smietana, "Bill Hybels Accused of Sexual Misconduct by Former Willow Creek Leaders," *Christianity Today*, March 22, 2018, www.christianitytoday .com/news/2018/march/bill-hybels-misconduct-willow-creek-john-nancy -ortberg.html.

2. Bob Allen, "Paige Patterson claims First Amendment defense in abuse lawsuit," *Baptist News Global*, August 27, 2019, https://baptistnews.com/article/paige -patterson-claims-first-amendment-defense-in-abuse-lawsuit/# .XWpcf5NKgn1. Boldface added for emphasis.

3. Boz Tchividjian, speech at the Southern Baptist Convention's Caring Well Conference, October 3, 2019. Tchividjian also gave the authors access to his typed and handwritten notes. A video recording of the speech may be found online at www.facebook.com/flyingfreenow/videos/1136635310058916.

4. Jim Van Yperen, "How Can a Church Witness Well in the Aftermath of Sexual Abuse?" Misio Alliance, February 28, 2018, www.missioalliance.org/can -church-witness-well-aftermath-sexual-abuse.

5. Van Yperen, "How Can a Church Witness Well," adapted.

6. Robert Cunningham, Twitter thread on November 17, 2017, https://twitter.com /tcpcrobert/status/931539423010975744.

7. Robert Cunningham, "Addressing Our Past," Tates Creek Presbyterian Church, June 24, 2018, https://tcpca.org/addressing-our-past.

8. Cunningham, "Addressing Our Past."

9. Morgan Eads, "Lexington Church Releases Findings of Investigation into Ex-pastor Accused of Rubbing Feet," *Lexington Herald Leader*, June 10, 2019, www .kentucky.com/news/local/counties/fayette-county/article231381283.html.

10. Cunningham, "Addressing Our Past."

11. Cunningham, "Addressing Our Past."

12. Cunningham, "Addressing Our Past."

13. Cunningham, "Addressing Our Past." Italics added.

14. Robert Cunningham, "Addressing Our Present & Future," Tates Creek Presbyterian Church, June 8, 2019, https://tcpca.org/addressing-our-present -future?fbclid=IwAR2RQVocpSiZeNKrE1NQelRASWKm _DGLi57LTmyYk5hGRqUlbb2KIbbIOWc.

15. English translations vary here: The Greek term is "brother" or "sibling" so "member of the church" is a reasonable translation.

16. The misuse of Matthew 18 is an example of *institutional betrayal*, seen here as an attempt to punish victims and whistleblowers. To read more about institutional betrayal, see Carly Parnitzke Smith and Jennifer J. Freyd, "Institutional Betrayal," *American Psychologist* 69, no. 6, September 2014, 575–587; https://dynamic.uoregon.edu/jjf/articles/sf2014.pdf.

17. "04-10-18 Willow Creek Bill Hybels Early Retirement Mtg," Brandy Bo Bandy YouTube channel, www.youtube.com/watch?v=H1M6atmmFe8, 21:43–21:53.

18. Vonda Dyer, conversation with the authors, January 4, 2020.

19. Jennifer Babich, "Why 2 Women Are Speaking Up about Pastoral Abuse 17 Years after Being Told to Stay Silent," Clarksville, *Leaf Chronicle*, November 7, 2019, www.theleafchronicle.com/story/news/2019/11/05/first-baptist -clarksville-pastor-abuse-wes-feltner-berean-baptist-claims/4158696002.

20. Chris Smith, "Pastor Resigns After Abuse Allegations Derailed Hiring by First Baptist Clarksville," Clarksville, *Leaf Chronicle*, November 26, 2019, https:// www.theleafchronicle.com/story/news/local/clarksville/2019/11/26/pastoral -abuse-candidate-rejected-first-baptist-resigns/4311127002.

21. NIV

22. "Anne Marie Miller's Victim Impact Statement after Guilty Plea from Mark Aderholt and Other Women Come Forward," http://annemariemiller.com/2019 /07/02/anne-marie-millers-victim-impact-statement-after-guilty-plea-from -mark-aderholt-and-other-women-come-forward/?preview=true; "I Was

Assaulted. He Was Applauded," *New York Times*, March 9, 2018, www.nytimes
.com/2018/03/09/opinion/jules-woodson-andy-savage-assault.html.
23. 1 Corinthians 6:1, 5-6, NIV
24. Robert Carl Mickens, quoted in Frédéric Martel, *In the Closet of the Vatican*,
trans. Shaun Whiteside (London: Bloomsbury Continuum, 2019), 423.

CHAPTER 4: FALSE NARRATIVES

1. I (Scot) first started compiling a list of false narratives while reading a study
of how the Lutheran churches in Germany responded after World War II as
the realities of the Holocaust were revealed. I recommend reading Matthew
D. Hockenos, *A Church Divided: German Protestants Confront the Nazi Past*
(Bloomington, IN: Indiana University Press, 2004). See also Boz Tchividjian,
"False Narratives of Christian Leaders Caught in Abuse," *Religion News Service*,
August 28, 2015, https://religionnews.com/2015/08/28/false-narratives-of
-christian-leaders-caught-in-abuse.
2. For more on "institutional betrayal," see Carly Parnitzke Smith and Jennifer
J. Freyd, "Institutional Betrayal," *American Psychologist* 69, no. 6, September
2014, 575–587, https://dynamic.uoregon.edu/jjf/articles/sf2014.pdf.
3. Morgan Lee, "My Larry Nassar Testimony Went Viral. But There's More to the
Gospel than Forgiveness," *Christianity Today*, January 31, 2018, www
.christianitytoday.com/ct/2018/january-web-only/rachael-denhollander-larry
-nassar-forgiveness-gospel.html. Italics added.
4. Nancy Beach, "My Response to the 'Apology,'" personal blog, May 11, 2018,
www.nancylbeach.com/blog/myresponsetotheapology.
5. Wade Burleson, "You Can't Forgive Foolishness: James MacDonald on 'Spiritual
Authority' Invested in the Church Elders," Istoria Ministries (blog), September
17, 2014, www.wadeburleson.org/2014/09/you-cant-forgive-foolishness-james
.html. Italics in the original.
6. Burleson, "You Can't Forgive Foolishness."
7. Keri Ladouceur, conversation with Laura McKnight Barringer, September 11,
2019.
8. "Prohibited Employment Policies/Practices," US Equal Employment
Opportunity Commission, www.eeoc.gov/laws/practices.
9. Keri Ladouceur, conversation.
10. "[Hybels] said he recalled not giving [Nancy] Beach latitude to do as much
teaching at Willow Creek as she might have liked but said he did not know
whether that had triggered her making allegations against him. Regardless, he
insisted he did nothing wrong. 'When (the allegation) surfaced in 2016, I was
like, no, who twisted that one?' Hybels told the Tribune." Quoted from Manya
Brachear Pashman and Jeff Coen, "After Years of Inquiries, Willow Creek
Pastor Denies Misconduct Allegations," *Chicago Tribune*, March 23, 2018,
https://www.chicagotribune.com/news/breaking/ct-met-willow-creek-pastor
-20171220-story.html.

11. Bill Hybels, quoted in Laurie Goodstein, "He's a Superstar Pastor. She Worked for Him and Says He Groped Her Repeatedly," *New York Times*, August 7, 2018, https://www.nytimes.com/2018/08/05/us/bill-hybels-willow-creek-pat -baranowski.html.

12. Betty Schmidt, "Shining the Light on the Truth," personal blog, April 10, 2018, https://veritasbetold.wixsite.com/website.

13. As of this writing, Willow Creek has not publicly apologized to Betty Schmidt, nor has the leadership corrected the ways in which it characterized her words.

14. "Gaslighting," Wikipedia, https://en.wikipedia.org/wiki/Gaslighting.

15. Paige L. Sweet, "The Sociology of Gaslighting," *American Sociological Review* 84, no. 5 (2019): 852, https://www.asanet.org/sites/default/files/attach/journals /oct19asrfeature.pdf.

16. Sweet, "The Sociology of Gaslighting."

17. Stephanie Sarkis, "Why Narcissists and Gaslighters Blatantly Lie—and Get Away with It," *Forbes*, June 2, 2019, www.forbes.com/sites/stephaniesarkis/2019 /06/02/why-narcissists-and-gaslighters-blatantly-lie-and-get-away-with-it /#7c68c84f43b0.

18. "Silent No More: A Survivor of Sexual Assault by Prominent Memphis Pastor Andy Savage Shares Her Story," *Watchkeep* (blog), January 5, 2018, http:// watchkeep.blogspot.com/2018/01/silent-no-more-survivor-of-sexual.html.

19. "03-23-18 Willow Response to Hybels Allegations Pt 1," Brandy Bo Bandy YouTube channel, www.youtube.com/watch?v=ojmS_uEhQRo, 9:45–10:35.

20. Pam Orr, quoted in Bob Smietana, "Bill Hybels Accused of Sexual Misconduct by Former Willow Creek Leaders," *Christianity Today*, March 22, 2018, www .christianitytoday.com/news/2018/march/bill-hybels-misconduct-willow -creek-john-nancy-ortberg.html.

21. "03-23-18 Willow Response to Hybels Allegations Pt 1," 11:13–11:39. Italics added to capture inflection of spoken statements.

22. Nancy Beach, "Why We Can't Move On," personal blog, April 11, 2018, www .nancylbeach.com/blog/2018/4/11/why-we-cant-move-on.

23. "Defendant Fails to Uncover Desired Scandal, Opting to Publish Old Gossip," Harvest Bible Chapel, December 13, 2018, www.harvestbiblechapel.org/2018/12 /13/defendant-fails-to-uncover-scandal.

24. Wade Mullen, "Deciphering the Language of Harvest Bible Chapel," *Medium*, February 20, 2019, https://medium.com/@wademullen/deciphering-the -language-of-harvest-bible-chapel-4a88fa0f83d7.

25. Mullen, "Deciphering the Language of Harvest."

26. Mullen, "Deciphering the Language of Harvest."

27. Rachel Held Evans, "How [Not to] Respond to Abuse Allegations: Christians and Sovereign Grace Ministries," personal blog, February 28, 2013, https:// rachelheldevans.com/blog/sovereign-grace-ministries-abuse-allegations.

28. Mark Galli, "We Need an Independent Investigation of Sovereign Grace Ministries," *Christianity Today*, March 22, 2018, www.christianitytoday.com

/ct/2018/march-web-only/sovereign-grace-need-investigation-sgm-mahaney
-denhollander.html.

29. Mary DeMuth, Twitter, September 3, 2019, https://twitter.com/MaryDeMuth
/status/1168990090829422595.

30. "Bylaws: 10.4 Formal Dispute Resolution," The Village Church, https://
thevillagechurch.net/about/beliefs/bylaws/#10.4. Italics added.

31. Elizabeth Dias, "Her Evangelical Megachurch Was Her World. Then Her
Daughter Said She Was Molested by a Minister," New York Times, June 10, 2019,
www.nytimes.com/2019/06/10/us/southern-baptist-convention-sex-abuse.html.

32. Dias, "Her Evangelical Megachurch."

33. Dias, "Her Evangelical Megachurch."

34. Elizabeth Dias, "An Evangelical Megachurch Is Sued for More Than $1 Million
in Child Sexual Abuse Case," New York Times, July 26, 2019, nytimes.com/2019
/07/26/us/village-church-texas-sexual-abuse-lawsuit.html.

35. Elizabeth Dias, "Her Evangelical Megachurch."

36. Mitch Little, text message to Scot McKnight, July 3, 2019.

37. Julie Roys, "Hard Times at Harvest," World magazine, December 13, 2018,
https://world.wng.org/2018/12/hard_times_at_harvest.

38. Jennifer Babich, "Why 2 Women Are Speaking Up about Pastoral Abuse 17 Years
after Being Told to Stay Silent," Clarksville (TN) Leaf-Chronicle, November 5,
2019, www.theleafchronicle.com/story/news/2019/11/05/first-baptist-clarksville
-pastor-abuse-wes-feltner-berean-baptist-claims/4158696002.

39. John Bacon, "Pope: Answer Those Who 'Only Seek Scandal' with Silence, Prayer,"
USA Today, September 3, 2018, www.usatoday.com/story/news/world/2018/09
/03/pope-answer-those-who-only-seek-scandal-silence-prayer/1184690002.

40. Bacon, "Pope."

41. Rome Reports, "Pope Francis at Santa Marta: Respond to People Only Seeking
Destruction with Silence," YouTube, September 3, 2018, www.youtube.com
/watch?time_continue=53&v=haTEtxImNiQ&feature=emb_title, 0:53–1:08.

42. Keri Ladouceur, conversation.

43. "03-23-18 Willow Response to Hybels Allegations Pt 1," 52:36–52:46. Italics
added to capture inflection of spoken statements.

44. "03-23-18 Willow Response," 47:52–48:25.

45. "03-23-18 Willow Response," 44:38–46:56.

46. Nancy Ortberg, "Flawed Process, Wounded Women," personal blog, April 12,
2018, www.nancylortberg.com.

47. Ortberg, "Flawed Process."

48. "Sovereign Grace Churches Will Not Seek an Independent Investigation into
Abuse Allegations," Relevant, April 16, 2019, https://relevantmagazine.com
/god/church/sovereign-grace-churches-will-not-seek-an-independent
-investigation-into-abuse-allegations.

49. Wade Mullen, "What I've Observed When Institutions Try to Apologize and

How They Can Do Better," personal blog, July 19, 2019, https://wademullen
.xyz/2019/07/19/institutional-apologies.

50. Mullen, "What I've Observed."
51. Mullen, "What I've Observed."
52. Mullen, "What I've Observed."
53. Mullen, "What I've Observed."
54. Mullen, "What I've Observed."

CHAPTER 5: CREATING A GOODNESS CULTURE

1. Luke 11:34-36
2. Scot McKnight, "Willow: Why the Women Went Public?" *Jesus Creed* (blog),
   July 9, 2018, https://www.patheos.com/blogs/jesuscreed/2018/07/09/willow
   -why-the-women-went-public.
3. Romans 3:12, KJV
4. Romans 3:10-12, 17-18, adapted from the NLT.
5. Romans 12:21; Galatians 6:9; Ephesians 2:10; 1 Thessalonians 5:15;
   2 Thessalonians 3:13; 2 Timothy 3:17; Titus 3:8; Hebrews 13:16, 20-21; James
   3:13, 1 Peter 3:11
6. Galatians 5:22
7. Goodness is an "executive" virtue, one that governs all behavior and cannot
   be narrowed to one specific command or prohibition. A good person is one
   who has discerned what is good and does good repeatedly over time. For an
   insightful study of goodness, see Christopher J. H. Wright, *Cultivating the
   Fruit of the Spirit: Growing in Christlikeness* (Downers Grove, IL: IVP, 2017),
   especially pages 97–112.
8. Amos 5:14-15
9. Psalm 119:68
10. Exodus 33:19
11. Joshua 21:45
12. Psalm 23:6
13. Psalm 34:8
14. Psalm 73:28
15. Psalm 86:5
16. Genesis 1:2
17. The Greek translation of *tov* in Genesis 1 is *kalos*, which means "excellent" and
    "beautiful."
18. Mark 12:28-32
19. See Scot McKnight, *The Jesus Creed: Loving God, Loving Others*, 2nd edition
    (Paraclete, 2019).
20. Acts 10:38, italics added.
21. 1 Kings 8:36, NRSV
22. Luke 6:35; Matthew 7:17-19
23. Galatians 5:22

24. Romans 15:14
25. Ephesians 5:9, NIV, italics added.
26. Here are some major examples: My two favorites are Galatians 6:9-10 and Romans 12:9. See also the following in the NIV: 2 Corinthians 9:9; Colossians 1:10; 2 Thessalonians 3:13; and then especially in Paul's pastoral letter to Titus: Titus 1:8; 2:3, 7, 13-14; 3:1-2, 8, 14.
27. NIV, italics added.
28. Italics added.
29. "Virginia Coach Bennett Rejects Raise in New Deal," ESPN, September 16, 2019, https://www.espn.com/mens-college-basketball/story/_/id/27629534/virginia-bennett-rejects-raise-new-deal.
30. Ephesians 2:10, italics added.
31. 1 Peter 2:15, NIV. See also 1 Peter 2:20; 3:11, 17, NIV.
32. 1 Peter 4:19, NIV
33. 1 Peter 2:13-14, NIV
34. Galatians 5:19-20, NIV
35. Genesis 2:9
36. Genesis 3:5
37. Isaiah 7:15-16
38. Isaiah 56:2
39. Jeremiah 7:24
40. Psalm 37:27
41. Matthew 3:17, NIV
42. Matthew 25:21, 23; Luke 19:17
43. Luke 23:50
44. Nearly sixty times in the Septuagint, the Greek translation of the Hebrew Bible, the Greek word *eu* translates the Hebrew *tov*. For example, in Deuteronomy 5:16 (NIV), we are told to honor our parents "that it may go well [*tov* in Hebrew, *eu* in Greek] with you."
45. See, for instance, Matthew 8:2-4.
46. Matthew 8:3, 16; Matthew 9:4, 10
47. Matthew 9:35
48. Matthew 5:3-12

CHAPTER 6: *TOV* CHURCHES NURTURE EMPATHY
1. Luke 4:18-19, NRSV, italics added.
2. Perches Funeral Home Facebook post, August 13, 2019, https://www.facebook.com/PerchesFuneralHome/photos/a.1347174618643225/2867142816646390/?type=3&theater.
3. Audra D. S. Burch, "In El Paso, Hundreds Show Up to Mourn a Woman They Didn't Know," *New York Times*, August 16, 2019, https://www.nytimes.com/2019/08/16/us/el-paso-funeral-basco.html.
4. Tal Axelrod, "Hundreds Join Widower to Attend Funeral of El Paso Shooting

Victim," *The Hill*, August 16, 2019, https://thehill.com/blogs/blog-briefing-room/news/457793-hundreds-attend-funeral-of-el-paso-shooting-victim-after.

5. "Supporting Margie Reckard Family," GoFundMe, created August 7, 2019, https://www.gofundme.com/f/1pvhtdot9c?stop=1.

6. Adolfo Flores, "His Wife Died in the El Paso Shooting and He Has No Other Family, So Hundreds Showed Up for Her Funeral," *BuzzFeed News*, August 17, 2019, https://www.buzzfeednews.com/article/adolfoflores/el-paso-funeral-man-no-family-antonio-basco-margie-reckard

7. Beverly Engel, "What Is Compassion and How Can It Improve My Life?," *Psychology Today*, April 29, 2008, https://www.psychologytoday.com/us/blog/the-compassion-chronicles/200804/what-is-compassion-and-how-can-it-improve-my-life.

8. Beth Moore has correlated patriarchal complementarianism with the abuse of women in the church. We believe she is right to do so. See Leah MarieAnn Klett, "Beth Moore Answers: Does Complementarian Theology Cause Abuse within the Church?," *Christian Post*, October 6, 2019, https://www.christianpost.com/news/beth-moore-answers-does-complementarian-theology-cause-abuse-within-the-church.html

9. Jen Pollock Michel, "A Message to John MacArthur: The Bible Calls Both Men and Women to 'Go Home,'" *Christianity Today*, October 24, 2019, https://www.christianitytoday.com/ct/2019/october-web-only/john-macarthur-bible-invites-both-men-women-go-home.html.

10. "Memorial to the Women of World War II," *Atlas Obscura*, https://www.atlasobscura.com/places/memorial-to-the-women-of-world-war-ii.

11. Memorial designer John Mills, quoted in "Memorial to the Women of World War II."

12. Again, we're focusing on women, but what we say here applies to every sister or brother who has ever been marginalized, wounded, or silenced, or who has become nameless, faceless, and formless in the church. The point of a *tov* culture is that *everyone* feels honored and valued and that they have a voice.

13. Laceye C. Warner, *Saving Women : Retrieving Evangelistic Theology and Practice* (Waco, TX: Baylor University Press, 2007), 223.

14. Warner, *Saving Women*, 224.

15. Mary McLeod Bethune, "Closed Doors (1936)," in *Mary McLeod Bethune: Building a Better World*, Audrey Thomas McCluskey and Elaine M. Smith, eds. (Bloomington, IN: Indiana University Press, 1999), 211.

CHAPTER 7: *TOV* CHURCHES NURTURE GRACE

1. Harold L. Senkbeil, *The Care of Souls: Cultivating a Pastor's Heart* (Bellingham, WA: Lexham Press, 2019), 24–25.

2. 1 John 4:18, NIV

3. John M. G. Barclay, *Paul and the Gift* (Grand Rapids: Eerdmans, 2015), 6, 575.

4. Colossians 2:14

5. Matthew 23:8-9

6. Galatians 3:28

7. James D. G. Dunn, *The Acts of the Apostles*, Narrative Commentaries (Valley Forge, PA: Trinity Press International, 1966), 12.

8. C. S. Lewis, *Mere Christianity* (New York: Macmillan, 1943), 104.

9. 1 John 4:18, NIV

CHAPTER 8: *TOV* CHURCHES NURTURE A PEOPLE-FIRST CULTURE

1. Fred Rogers, "I Give an Expression of Care Every Day to Each Child," *Current*, May 2, 1969, https://current.org/1969/05/i-give-an-expression-of-care-every -day-to-each-child/.

2. Maxwell King, *The Good Neighbor: The Life and Work of Fred Rogers* (New York: Abrams Press, 2018), 317–318.

3. Tom Junod, quoted in Maxwell King, *The Good Neighbor*, 305.

4. King, *The Good Neighbor*, 202.

5. King, *The Good Neighbor*, 9.

6. Mitch Randall, "Theological Malpractice Stands Culpable in Sexual Abuse," EthicsDaily.com, August 15, 2019, https://ethicsdaily.com/theological -malpractice-stands-culpable-in-sexual-abuse/.

7. Randall, "Theological Malpractice."

8. Luke 6:31

9. Adapted from David Brooks, *The Second Mountain: The Quest for a Moral Life* (New York: Random House, 2019), 60–62

10. Adapted from Brooks, *Second Mountain*, 62.

11. Communities In Schools website, "About Us: Our History," www .communitiesinschools.org/about-us.

12. Genesis 1:26

13. Genesis 1:26, NIV

14. Colossians 1:15

15. NLT

16. NRSV

17. 1 Corinthians 6:11

18. Philemon 1:16, NIV, italics added.

19. Galatians 3:28

20. Matthew 9:36; 14:14; Mark 1:41

21. Paula Gooder, *Everyday God: The Spirit of the Ordinary* (Minneapolis: Fortress, 2015), 57.

22. Colossians 1:28–2:2

CHAPTER 9: *TOV* CHURCHES NURTURE TRUTH

1. Matthew 18:3, NIV

2. 1 Timothy 2:3-4

3. 1 Timothy 3:15

4. John 1:14, NIV, italics added.
5. John 14:6, italics added.
6. C. S. Lewis, *The Lion, the Witch and the Wardrobe* (New York: HarperCollins, 1950), 67-68.
7. John 15:26; 16:13
8. 1 John 5:6
9. 1 Corinthians 13:6, NIV
10. 2 Corinthians 6:4, 7, NIV
11. Ephesians 4:25, NIV
12. Ephesians 6:14, NIV
13. 1 John 1:6, NIV
14. Miroslav Volf and Matthew Croasmun, *For the Life of the World: Theology That Makes a Difference* (Grand Rapids: Brazos, 2019), 137.
15. Vonda Dyer, No More Silence conference, Dallas Theological Seminary, September 9, 2019, www.youtube.com/watch?v=tBeGmwW5-v0, 5:50–7:18.
16. John 1:9, NIV
17. John 3:21
18. John 8:32
19. Ephesians 5:8-9, NIV
20. Romans 1:18
21. James 3:14
22. Mike Breaux, "Journey through John: Come and See," sermon at Willow Creek Community Church, January 27, 2019, www.youtube.com/watch?v=ISjXhWUyGi0, 19:51–20:06, 20:29–20:36, 22:12–22:21, 25:08–25:20, 25:48–25:56, 26:07–26:12.
23. Keri Ladouceur, conversation with Laura McKnight Barringer, September 11, 2019.
24. See Jeremiah 19:1-13.
25. See Jeremiah 13:1-11.
26. Leviticus 23:26-32. See also Leviticus 16; Numbers 29:7-11.
27. James 5:16; 1 John 1:8-10
28. Dietrich Bonhoeffer, *Discipleship*, Dietrich Bonhoeffer Works, vol. 4, trans. Barbara Green and Reinhard Krauss (Minneapolis: Fortress, 2001), 43–44.
29. Steve Carter, "A Diverging Path," personal blog, August 5, 2018, www.steveryancarter.com/post/a-diverging-path.
30. Carter, "Diverging Path."
31. "James MacDonald Harvest Bible Chapel Excommunication," Internet Archive, September 19, 2013, https://archive.org/details/JamesMacDonaldHarvastBibleChapel, 3:28–3:33.
32. Willow Creek Elder Board, "Elder Update and Worship & Reflection Service," July 19, 2019, www.willowcreek.org/en/blogs/south-barrington/elder-update-july-19-2019.
33. Willow Creek Elder Board, "Elder Update."

34. Willow Creek Elder Board, "Elder Update."
35. Willow Creek Elder Board, "Elder Update."
36. See, for example, Nancy Beach, "The Morning After the 'Final Willow Meeting," personal blog, July 24, 2019, www.nancylbeach.com/blog/2019 /7/24/the-morning-after-the-final-willow-meeting.
37. Shoji Boldt, Willow Creek Community Church Elder-led Worship & Reflection Service, July 23, 2019. Video embedded in Willow Creek Elder Board, "Elder Update and Worship & Reflection Service," July 19, 2019, www.willowcreek .org/en/blogs/south-barrington/elder-update-july-19-2019, 27:19–27:28.
38. Silvia Escobar, Willow Creek Community Church Elder-led Worship & Reflection Service, July 23, 2019. Video embedded in Willow Creek Elder Board, "Elder Update and Worship & Reflection Service," July 19, 2019, www .willowcreek.org/en/blogs/south-barrington/elder-update-july-19-2019, 35:35–35:37.
39. 2 Corinthians 5:18, NIV
40. Wade Mullen, Twitter, July 25, 2019, twitter.com/wademullen/status /1154408308331208706.
41. James Baldwin, "The Creative Process," in *The Price of the Ticket: Collected Nonfiction, 1948–1985* (New York: St. Martin's Press, 1985), 318.
42. Baldwin, "Creative Process."
43. Adapted from Baldwin, "The Creative Process." Baldwin's original statement is as follows: "We have an opportunity that no other nation has of moving beyond the Old World concepts of race and class and caste, to create, finally, what we must have had in mind when we first began speaking of the New World."

CHAPTER 10: *TOV* CHURCHES NURTURE JUSTICE

1. Maya Salam, "How Larry Nassar 'Flourished Unafraid' for So Long," *New York Times*, May 3, 2019, www.nytimes.com/2019/05/03/sports/larry-nassar -gymnastics-hbo-doc.html.
2. Beth LeBlanc and Matt Mencarini, "Rachael Denhollander, First to Publicly Accuse Nassar, Makes Final Victim Statement," *Lansing State Journal*, January 24, 2018, https://www.lansingstatejournal.com/story/news/local/2018/01/24 /denhollander-seeks-harsh-sentence-answers-tough-questions-nassar -sentencing/1060121001/.
3. "Read Rachael Denhollander's full victim impact statement about Larry Nassar," CNN, January 30, 2018, www.cnn.com/2018/01/24/us/rachael -denhollander-full-statement. See also, "Rachael Denhollander Delivers Powerful Final Victim Speech to Larry Nassar," YouTube, January 24, 2018, www.youtube.com/watch?v=7CjVOLToRJk.
4. Sovereign Grace Churches was previously known as Sovereign Grace Ministries. Sometimes the titles are used interchangeably.
5. "Read Rachael Denhollander's full victim impact statement."
6. Though Rachael Denhollander does not identify the leader's name in her

memoir, the *Washington Post* identifies him as C. J. Mahaney. Mahaney was attempting a return to ministry after a class-action lawsuit alleged that he covered up sexual abuse at SGC. Immanuel Baptist supported Mahaney's return to ministry, despite knowing he had never acknowledged his failure to properly handle sexual abuse allegations. See also Joshua Pease, "The Sin of Silence," *Washington Post*, May 31, 2018, www.washingtonpost.com/news /posteverything/wp/2018/05/31/feature/the-epidemic-of-denial-about-sexual -abuse-in-the-evangelical-church/.

7. Rachael Denhollander, *What Is a Girl Worth?* (Carol Stream, IL: Tyndale Momentum, 2019), 146.

8. Tiffany Stanley, "The Sex-Abuse Scandal That Devastated a Suburban Megachurch," *Washingtonian*, February 14, 2016, www.washingtonian .com/2016/02/14/the-sex-abuse-scandal-that-devastated-a-suburban -megachurch-sovereign-grace-ministries.

9. Sovereign Grace Staff, "FAQ Concerning Allegations against Sovereign Grace Churches," April 12, 2019, https://sovereigngrace.com/faq.

10. Morgan Lee, "My Larry Nassar Testimony Went Viral. But There's More to the Gospel than Forgiveness," *Christianity Today*, January 31, 2018, www .christianitytoday.com/ct/2018/january-web-only/rachael-denhollander-larry -nassar-forgiveness-gospel.html.

11. Denhollander, *What Is a Girl Worth?*, 58.

12. Denhollander, *What Is a Girl Worth?*, 306.

13. Denhollander, *What Is a Girl Worth?*, 146–148.

14. Lee, "My Larry Nassar Testimony."

15. Denhollander, *What Is a Girl Worth?*, 141.

16. G. A. Pritchard, *Willow Creek Seeker Services: Evaluating a New Way of Doing Church* (Grand Rapids: Baker, 1996), 43.

17. Dean Butters, "My Harvest Bible Chapel Story," January 29, 2019: 4, https:// wonderingeagle.files.wordpress.com/2019/03/dbutters-hbc-story.pdf.

18. Julie Roys, "Hard Times at Harvest," *World* magazine, December 13, 2018, https://world.wng.org/2018/12/hard_times_at_harvest.

19. Matthew 5:20

20. Ephesians 2:8-10

21. See Galatians 5:13-26.

22. James 1:27, NIV

23. James 2:1-9

24. This account adapted from Matthew D. Hockenos, *Then They Came for Me: Martin Niemöller, the Pastor Who Defied the Nazis* (New York: Basic Books, 2018), and Harold Marcuse, "The Origin and Reception of Martin Niemöller's Quotation 'First They Came for the Communists . . . ,'" (July 31, 2014), http:// marcuse.faculty.history.ucsb.edu/publications/articles /Marcuse2016OriginReceptionNiemoellersQuotationOcr.pdf.

25. For a discussion of the evolution of Niemöller's lines, see Marcuse, "The Origin and Reception of Martin Niemöller's Quotation."

26. Here's a little-known story, told in Hockenos, *Then They Came for Me*: While in prison in 1937, Niemöller received a copy of Bonhoeffer's now-famous text *The Cost of Discipleship* with an inscription from Bonhoeffer: "To Pastor Martin Niemöller at Advent 1937 in brotherly thanks. A book that he himself could have written better than the author."

CHAPTER 11: *TOV* CHURCHES NURTURE SERVICE

1. Ephesians 4:11-13, NIV
2. Hebrews 10:24
3. Mark 10:42-45
4. Matthew 19:21
5. Matthew 6:2, NIV
6. Matthew 6:3-4
7. Calvin Miller, *Life Is Mostly Edges: A Memoir* (Nashville: Thomas Nelson, 2008), 58–59.
8. See Kathleen Norris, *The Quotidian Mysteries: Laundry, Liturgy and "Women's Work"* (New York: Paulist, 1998).
9. Paula Gooder, *Everyday God: The Spirit of the Ordinary* (Minneapolis: Fortress, 2015), x.
10. Dallas Willard, *Life without Lack: Living in the Fullness of Psalm 23* (Nashville: Nelson Books, 2018), 58.
11. John Ortberg, in the afterword of Gary W. Moon, *Becoming Dallas Willard: The Formation of a Philosopher, Teacher, and Christ Follower* (Downers Grove, IL: IVP, 2018), 255–256.
12. Ralph E. Enlow Jr., *Servant of All: Reframing Greatness and Leadership through the Teachings of Jesus* (Bellingham, WA: Kirkdale Press, 2019), 67–68.
13. James C. Galvin, *Willow Creek Governance Review, 2014–2018*, April 14, 2019: 3, https://gallery.mailchimp.com/dfd0f4e0c107728235d2ff080/files/6d3bafc4 -0b43-450c-8e1e-4eb1c80771e2/Report_on_Governance_Review_2014_2018 _FINAL.pdf.
14. Mary DeMuth, "10 Ways to Spot Spiritual Abuse," *Restory* (personal website), September 6, 2016, www.marydemuth.com/spiritual-abuse-10-ways-to-spot-it. Italics in the original.
15. Amy Simpson, "When Moral Boundaries Become Incubators for Sin," *Christianity Today*, March 25, 2019, www.christianitytoday.com/pastors/2019 /march-web-exclusives/when-moral-boundaries-become-incubators-for-sin .html.
16. Andy Crouch, "It's Time to Reckon with Celebrity Power," TGC, March 24, 2018, www.thegospelcoalition.org/article/time-reckon-celebrity-power.
17. Chuck DeGroat, *When Narcissism Comes to Church: Healing Your Community from Emotional and Spiritual Abuse* (Downers Grove, IL: IVP, 2020), 82.

18. Kate Bowler, *The Preacher's Wife: The Precarious Power of Evangelical Women Celebrities* (Princeton, NJ: Princeton University Press, 2019), xiii.
19. Bowler, *Preacher's Wife*, xv.
20. Paul Simon, "The Sound of Silence," lyrics © Universal Music Publishing Group, BMG Rights Management.
21. Matthew 23:5-7
22. Romans 16:12; 1 Corinthians 3:9, NIV; 1 Corinthians 4:13, NIV
23. Mark 10:32-34, NIV
24. Scripture quotations in this section adapted from Mark 10:33-40, NIV.
25. Mark 10:42-45, NIV
26. Miller, *Life Is Mostly Edges*, 351.
27. Miller, *Life Is Mostly Edges*, 351–352.
28. Mike Glenn, *Coffee with Mom: Caring for a Parent with Dementia* (Nashville: B&H, 2019), 2, 48–50.
29. Romans 12:3, NIV
30. K. Patricia Cross, abstract for "Not *Can*, but *Will* College Teaching Be Improved?," *New Directions for Higher Education* 1977, no. 17 (Spring 1977): 1, https://onlinelibrary.wiley.com/doi/abs/10.1002/he.36919771703.

CHAPTER 12: *TOV* CHURCHES NURTURE CHRISTLIKENESS

1. David Brooks, *The Second Mountain: The Quest for a Moral Life* (New York: Random House, 2019), 23.
2. Brooks, *Second Mountain*, 23. Italics added.
3. Brooks, *Second Mountain*, 23. Italics added.
4. Brooks, *Second Mountain*, 22.
5. Willow Creek Community Church, Senior Pastor job description, www .vanderbloemen.com/job/willow-creek-community-church-senior-pastor. This job description was taken down after Willow Creek announced the hiring of a new senior pastor on April 15, 2020. Last accessed by the authors on March 26, 2020.
6. Willow Creek Community Church, Senior Pastor job description.
7. Willow Creek Community Church, Senior Pastor job description. Italics added.
8. Eugene Peterson, *Working the Angles: The Shape of Pastoral Integrity* (Grand Rapids: Eerdmans, 1993), 3.
9. Eugene Peterson, *The Pastor: A Memoir* (New York: HarperOne, 2011), 5. This theme runs throughout *The Pastor*.
10. The following re-expresses what I (Scot) have written in my book *Pastor Paul: Nurturing a Culture of Christoformity in the Church* (Baker, 2019).
11. Eugene Peterson, *The Contemplative Pastor: Returning to the Art of Spiritual Direction* (Grand Rapids: Eerdmans, 1989), 112–116.
12. Eugene H. Peterson, "Pastor Paul," in *Romans and the People of God: Essays in Honor of Gordon D. Fee on the Occasion of His 65th Birthday*, Sven K. Soderlund and N. T. Wright, eds. (Grand Rapids: Eerdmans, 1999), 283–294 (here p. 291).

13. 2 Corinthians 11:28
14. Acts 20:31
15. 2 Corinthians 2:12-13
16. 2 Corinthians 7:2
17. Romans 11:1-31; Ephesians 2:11–3:6
18. 1 John 4:16-18, italics added.
19. Philippians 2:5-11, NIV
20. Romans 8:29
21. 1 Corinthians 12–14
22. Galatians 5:13-25
23. Teresa Morgan, *Every-Person Ministry: Reaching out in Christ* (London: SPCK, 2011), 4–5.
24. See Patrick Kiefert, Wesley Granberg-Michaelson, *How Change Comes to Your Church: A Guidebook for Church Innovations* (Grand Rapids: Eerdmans, 2019).
25. Adapted from Keifert and Granberg-Michaelson, *How Change Comes*, 23–24.

ABOUT THE AUTHORS

SCOT McKNIGHT is the Julius R. Mantey Professor of New Testament at Northern Seminary and a recognized authority on the New Testament, early Christianity, and the historical Jesus. He is the author of more than 80 books, including the award-winning *The Jesus Creed* as well as *The King Jesus Gospel, A Fellowship of Differents, The Blue Parakeet,* and *Kingdom Conspiracy.* He maintains a blog at christianitytoday.com/scot-mcknight. He and his wife, Kristen, live in the northwest suburbs of Chicago, where they enjoy long walks, gardening, and cooking.

LAURA BARRINGER is a teacher of first and second grade students. She is coauthor of *Sharing God's Love: The Jesus Creed for Children* and wrote a teacher lesson and activity guide to accompany the book. Laura is a graduate of Wheaton College and currently resides in the northwest suburbs of Chicago with her husband, Mark, and three beagles.